The Feminine Factor

The Feminine Factor

Eric Mount, Jr.

 **JOHN KNOX PRESS**
Richmond, Virginia

Library of Congress Cataloging in Publication Data

Mount, Eric.
  The feminine factor.

  Includes bibliographical references.
    1. Woman—History and condition of women.
  2. Women's Liberation Movement. I. Title.
  HQ1154.M72   301.41'2   72–11163
  ISBN 0–8042–0821–2

To
the futures of
Diane
Laurie
Marcia
Mary Faith
the memory of
Allison (1959–1960)

♀

A Straightforward Foreword

An Apology or a Confession?

I almost began by assuring you that I am not a "male chauvinist pig," but you'll draw your own conclusions anyway. And even if by some miracle I were as free of prejudice as we would all like to think we are, my involvement in and benefits from a sexist society make me a partner in crime at best. Asking myself whether I am ready to stay home with the children three and a half days a week or to accept gladly a political reversal in which the President of the United States, all the Cabinet, and 98 percent of the Congress were women[1] punctures any such smugness. And I could receive considerable discomfort from the revelations of one of the evening rituals at our house.

We were going through a period when even a national emergency would not deliver me from telling "Goldilocks and the Three Bears" and "The Three Little Pigs" before I could extricate myself from our three-year-old daughter's room. With repeated telling, more and more legendary accretions were added to embellish and "improve" the witnesses of the sources. It soon dawned on me that the activities and mannerisms we were attributing to Papa Bear, Mama Bear, and Baby (Boy) Bear were departing little from the stereotypes of the original. Of course, I could blame that on the story. The hurter came when we started assigning names to the three pigs who left home to seek their fortunes, and my daughter suggested Suzie in place of Porkie and Patti in place of Paul. I had, I realized, always assumed that the little porcine fortune hunters were male, and my daughter was not yet conditioned to reserve such ventures to boys. In our unexamined assumptions that "all the pigs are boys," it may be seen that "all the boys are pigs." And women who tell those stories are "male chauvinists" too in their perpetration of stereotypes.

Personal defenses aside, let me simply present myself as a married male religion professor and college pastor with four daughters who needs to sort some things out. I leave to others, past and future, the complete tracing of the history of masculine domination and of women's liberation. Others have also spared me the effort of covering all the church's positions and practices as regards sex and women. Other men have already spilled far too much ink on the perversities and excesses of the women's liberation movement when they could better have occupied themselves with why the whole business constitutes a threat to them and how they need liberating. I don't want to join them. I have to ask as a husband what the growing liberation of women means for the future shape of our marriage. I have to ask as the father of four girls what past errors in the rearing of girls I must correct or avoid and what cultural tendencies to limit their horizons or fulfillment I must attempt to counteract. I have to ask as a churchman who usually finds himself preaching to congregations (whether collegiate or conventional) numerically dominated by women what the church of the future must become if the authority and power of women is to be commensurate with their service and support and potentiality, and if the definitions of authority and power in the church are to undergo enough transformation to make women want to stay around even if they get a big piece of the action. I have to ask as a theologian what should and must happen to our theological stances largely developed by men when women are more involved in the theological enterprise and more considered as the bulk of the active laity to which significant theology must communicate. I have to ask as an ethicist what the moral ramifications of women's liberation are and what means should be employed to assure freedom and justice for all—women included. I have to ask what kind of future we are moving toward and what kind we want to move toward in the realm of sexual identity and roles. What is the wave of the future for my daughters? How should the future be shaped for them and for us all?

As I share some of the investigations and conjectures which have accompanied my attempts to sort out some of these questions, it will become apparent that what has emerged is a group of selective (or random, if you like) probes and inconclusive suggestions which do not add up to a comprehensive treatment of "Female and Male in the 1970's," and which will doubtless receive no more respect than their degree of certainty merits.

I hope the reader will peruse the following pages with the same spirit of openness and the same awareness of need to think new thoughts which I have tried to maintain in this preliminary wrestle with matters which will doubtless be concerning us deeply in the decade ahead, if it is to be women's equivalent of the 60's for blacks. Somewhat comforted by Gertrude Stein's assertion that it is better to ask questions than to give answers—even good ones—I dare to ask that you join voluntarily a quest which for the father of four daughters is more a necessity than a choice.

Acknowledgments

Although their enthusiasm about being identified with this effort probably varies from scant to none, more than a few friends have been of more than a little help on this book. Good friend, colleague, co-coach, and doubles partner Milton Scarborough first sent me to Erik Erikson's treatment of "Womanhood and Inner Space," and he also read and criticized a paper which was my first effort in these matters. Sallie TeSelle, editor of *Soundings*, was also of assistance in gathering comments and making improvements in the paper for publication. Several years ago, then-colleague Adam Fischer first suggested to me a difference in men's and women's perspectives on pornography. Reva Chrisman and Ben Feese, with whom I taught a course on human sexuality, and numerous students in that course and others have stimulated my thinking and broadened my range of inquiry. Centre College provided a research grant to support the preparation of the manuscript when I first expanded my explorations to book length in the summer of 1971. A former editor of John Knox Press, Davis Yeuell, encouraged me to produce a manuscript. The present editor, Richard Ray, and copy editor Dorothy Locke have been of immeasurable help in accomplishing the refinement of the manuscript. Annabel Girard, a neighbor, and Phyllis Emerson, veteran typist of my other book, have ably prepared the drafts. My family has tolerated the inconvenience my writing has brought them with laudable patience, and my dear wife, Truly, not only provided many helpful insights but also gave the manuscript a final reading. I thank them all, but you shouldn't blame any of them.

Contents

1

Blacks and Broads

Like Blacks, Like Broads

The parallels which have been drawn between the plight of black people and the plight of women are legion. Theodore Roszak has stated that "Women were indeed the first niggers in history—and are still apt to be the last liberated."[1] Both blacks and women are obviously distinguishable from the dominant group in ways that the Irish, the Jews, and the Italians, for instance, are not. Both are marked for discrimination by birth. Both have been called deficient in certain ways by nature. Both have had the shadowy sides of the psyches of the dominant group projected on them. Both have suffered the invisibility of being ignored and the anonymity of living vicariously through others. Both have developed degrees of deception, distrust, and apathy as a result of their victimization. Both have been blamed for their own victimization. Both have introjected many of the characteristics attributed to them so that the stereotypes have become self-fulfilling prophecies. Both have developed ploys for appeasing and even manipulating their masters. Both have been patronized and treated as children. Both have been asked to be comforted with the congratulation "You've come a long way, baby!" Both have supported a society which paid nothing or a lower scale for their labors. Both have been victimized by job ceilings (see statistics on women's employment as secretaries and blacks' as janitors as opposed to supervisory positions). Both have been urged to solve their problems as individuals rather than as a corporate movement. Both have suffered under the "Jackie Robinson syndrome," whereby the "Superblack" or "Superwoman" hurdles the barriers of discrimination and makes the grade on "Whitey's" or "Man's" turf and is then pointed to as an example of what "the rest of you could do if you really wanted to." Both have been asked to be satisfied by the sop of tokenism—maybe even by the same token. (The move of employers to fill two underdog quotas with one bone by hiring a black woman as a TV commentator or news reporter has been increasing recently.) Meanwhile the average black or girl or woman remains in one kind of ghetto or another. Both have turned fury toward their own group (see Fanon's analysis in *The Wretched of the Earth* of the violence of black people against black people) which is rooted in their hatred of the oppressors, who are unacceptable targets. Both have been offered the religious sop of a future where all God's children will be white and male or else truly equal. Both are now riding a second wave of effort and purpose which concerns itself more with the raising of consciousness or the establishment of identity and a revolution in the power relations and institutions of society than with the procuring of legal rights. Both have grown suspicious of coalition politics and come to insist on not being taken for granted by other liberationists. For both, I would venture, separatism cannot ultimately be a satisfactory solution, although it would appear to be more viable for blacks than for the sexes, as we shall see at the end of the chapter.

One of the classic comparisons is found in the following chart constructed by Helen Mayer Hacker.[2]

Castelike Status of Women and Negroes

NEGROES	WOMEN

1. High Social Visibility

a. Skin color, other "racial" characteristics	a. Secondary sex characteristics
b. (Sometimes) distinctive dress—bandana, flashy clothes	b. Distinctive dress, skirts, etc.

2. Ascribed Attributes

a. Inferior intelligence, smaller brain, less convoluted, scarcity of geniuses	a. ditto
b. More free in instinctual gratifications. More emotional, "primitive" and childlike. Imagined sexual prowess envied.	b. Irresponsible, inconsistent, emotionally unstable. Lack strong super-ego. Women as "temptresses."
c. Common stereotype, "inferior"	c. "Weaker"

3. Rationalizations of Status

a. Thought all right in his place	a. Woman's place is in the home
b. Myth of contented Negro	b. Myth of contented woman— "feminine" woman is happy in subordinate role

4. Accommodation Attitudes

a. Supplicatory whining intonation of voice	a. Rising inflection, smiles, laughs, downward glances
b. Deferential manner	b. Flattering manner
c. Concealment of real feelings	c. "Feminine wiles"
d. Outwit "white folks"	d. Outwit "men-folk"
e. Careful study of points at which dominant group is susceptible to influence	e. ditto
f. Fake appeals for directives; show of ignorance	f. Appearance of helplessness

5. Discriminations

a. Limitations on educa-tion—should fit "place" in society	a. ditto
b. Confined to traditional jobs—barred from supervisory positions. Their competition feared. No family precedents for new aspirations.	b. ditto
c. Deprived of political importance	c. ditto
d. Social and professional segregation	d. ditto
e. More vulnerable to criticism	e. e.g., conduct in bars [women drivers]

6. Similar Problems

a. Roles not clearly defined, but in flux as result of social change. Conflict between achieved status and ascribed status.

A more recent but almost as elaborate example is found in "Toward a Female Liberation Movement" by Beverly Jones and Judith Brown:

1. Women, like black slaves, belong to a master. They are property and whatever credit they gain redounds to him.
2. Women, like black slaves, have a personal relationship to the men who are their masters.
3. Women, like blacks, get their identity and status from white men.
4. Women, like blacks, play an idiot role in the theatre of the white man's fantasies. Though inferior and dumb, they are happy, especially when they can join a mixed group where they can mingle with The Man.
5. Women, like blacks, buttress the white man's ego. Needing such support, the white man fears its loss; fearing such loss, he fears women and blacks.
6. Women, like blacks, sustain the white man: "They wipe his ass and breast feed him when he is little, they school him in

his youthful years, do his clerical work and raise him and his replacements later, and all through his life in the factories, on the migrant farms, in the restaurants, hospitals, offices, and homes, they sew for him, stoop for him, cook for him, clean for him, sweep, run errands, haul away his garbage, and nurse him when his frail body alters."

7. Women, like blacks, are badly educated. In school they internalize a sense of being inferior, shoddy, and intellectually crippled. In general, the cultural apparatus—the profession of history, for example—ignores them.

8. Women, like blacks, see a Tom image of themselves in the mass media.

9. Striving women, like bourgeois blacks, become imitative, ingratiating, and materialistic when they try to make it in the white man's world.

10. Women, like blacks, suffer from the absence of any serious study on the possibility of real "temperamental and cognitive differences" between the races and the sexes.

11. The ambivalence of women toward marriage is like the ambivalence of blacks toward integration.[3]

Woman's internalization of male views of her has received some impressive documentation. The way blacks learned to view themselves through the white man's eyes and thus to look down on themselves has been supported by black children's choices of white dolls over black ones and illustrated in numerous other ways. Psychologist Philip Goldberg of Connecticut College has illustrated a similar self-negating tendency in an experiment with college women. Two booklets which contained the same series of articles in various professional fields, but which listed the authors as males in one case and as females in the other, were given to the women for evaluations of the value, style, and competence of the articles. The same article received significantly lower ratings when attributed to a woman. The largest difference was in traditionally masculine fields such as law or city planning; but even in elementary education and dietetics, the students rated the supposed work of males higher.[4]

The list of likenesses could be continued to great lengths,

and because such parallels are fruitful, it is suggestive to contemplate the responses of some ethicists to the black power movement since these might appropriately inform a Christian response to the various expressions of the women's liberation movement. It may be that we can avoid repeating some defensive backlashing if we draw some further parallels.

Bitches' Barks—Better Than Their Bites

The first consideration is that the biblical ethic has a definite bias toward the underdog. Old Testament concerns for the exploited poor, the widow, and the orphan continue into the New. Thus the church has been repeatedly reminded by Scripture that she should keep an ear open to the cries of those who have been exploited in any way, to the grievances of those who may be too powerless to gain justice unless others stand beside them.

Pointing to objectionable statements and actions on the part of an individual black militant or a group should not excuse us from listening for real grievances and what should be compelling claims for support. Admittedly these are sometimes covered with a deep layer of the ideological rhetoric that deals in absolutes and exaggerations, and delivered with a venom which does not stand up well under examination for unexceptionable accuracy or love of neighbor. However, the need for and value of civil rights marches or voter registration projects were not really dealt with by critics who cited the sexual practices of some in the movement. Furthermore, people getting involved in the struggle for racial equality have sometimes been warned that they would not like some of the people in places of leadership but that they must learn to get beyond personalities to issues. It has also proved oversimple to claim that a few militant and outspoken leaders really did not speak for most blacks. Certainly the polls showed that the bulk of the black populace identified more with the leadership of Martin Luther King than that, for instance, of H. Rap Brown, but the growth of black consciousness has made for a greater feeling of solidarity of the larger black community with more militant and less nonviolent leaders and groups, even though specific strategies or statements might be disapproved. "Whitey" is getting told and shown some things he needed to find out and straighten out, even if some black leaders are deemed too extreme by the average black. What is more, spokesmen who in the beginning perhaps spoke for a small percentage of blacks occasioned an awakened or heightened awareness of their grievances which had not previously been well enough defined to express or attack. For instance, Roy Wilkins has stated that he considers the Black Panthers his allies despite his disagreements with them. He acknowledges that the Panthers have a great deal more sympathy than the size of their membership (1,000 to 1,500) might indicate because they are complaining about things (injustice in the courts, police harassment, etc.) that blacks know to be true. As writers and speakers have reviewed the oppression of black people, these people have begun to understand the sources of their frustrations, to delineate the contours of their prisons, and to reckon the amount of their exploitation in much clearer ways than before.

In the case of the most strident advocates of women's liberation, people fool themselves when they write off one or another of these as a man-hater or a lesbian or a neurotic or a communist, or indulge in humor about their wristwatches being hidden by the hair on their arms. The fact that Kate Millett's father was continually asking her why she couldn't have been a boy certainly colors and even warps what she has to say, but it does not invalidate the whole of her message. The fact that she is admittedly bisexual certainly influences her outlook, but it does not justify writing her off because of what some might consider an abnormality.

The following exchange which Saul Bellow includes in *Mr. Sammler's Planet* reminds us that a distorted viewpoint does not preclude the possibility of any accurate vision:

> "You are a paranoiac, my dear fellow."
> "Perhaps, but that doesn't prevent people from plotting against me."[5]

Bellow observes, "That is an important ray of light from a dark source." This assertion is far too negative in its connotations for application to most spokesmen for either black liberation or women's liberation, but the point is that we in the Christian community must listen to what women are telling us. The church is obliged to give special attention to the barks and whines and whimpers of the underdog even if she's a bitch.

Every charge made and every solution offered in "women's lib" literature certainly will not be accepted by the critical hearer. Such blanket acceptance would of course be impossible even if it were desired, due to deep disagreements within the ranks of women's liberationists. Still, the assumption should be that the cries or shrieks or charges must be heard.

Some liberation literature is couched in Marxist rhetoric which is every bit as simplistic as some of the defensive rhetoric of the "corrupt capitalist society" which is attacked. Some of the programmatic insistences on the abolition of the institution of marriage deal in caricatures of that institution which at times render it all but unrecognizable. The touting of psyche castration as revenge for women's perennial rape is as morally repugnant as it is abhorrent to all but a few strident extremists. The male-hating broadsides of SCUM (the Society for Cutting Up Men) are a case in point. Still, Christians are obligated to a contrite consideration of why these liberationists should be so upset and what actual evils of the system we have perpetrated or accepted uncritically.

Beyond the ideological sloganizing and the snickered-at bra burnings lie critical social injustices and deep human needs to which a church that has been notoriously male-dominated must give serious heed. The Christian community has an imperative to care about woman's plight because it knows there is fire beneath the smoke about exploitation and domination of women.

If the women of the church listen it is quite possible that many more of them will come to be concerned about their liberation. And if the women of the church ever get their day in the courts of the church their raised consciousness of what it means to be an underdog might make them more sensitive to all kinds of captivities and oppressions. The vanguard of the feminists is apt to evoke a constituency of dissatisfaction and of determination to effect change even if it is not a constituency of agreement. Heightened sensitivity will grow out of the outspokenness of the militants. The drive toward sisterly solidarity is growing, and even those who ardently disavow being "women's libbers" add a "but" and list their gripes concerning women's shoddy treatment and unrealized potentialities.

A Bias Toward Freedom or a Barrier to It?

Not only must the church listen sympathetically because of who is speaking; she must listen with a positive predisposition toward what advocates of women's liberation are saying because of the content of their message. Such black theologians as James Cone have been pointing out to the church that liberation is not an implication of the gospel, it is the gospel. Theologians of revolution and advocates of "political theology" have also emphasized the biblical undergirding for the deliverance of man from all manner of political, social, and economic captivities. New Testament scholar Ernst Käsemann has written a volume entitled *Jesus Means Freedom.*

Jesus has to be seen as a liberator of men and women from powers that enslaved them. Examples are easy to name. His casting out of demons, his attack on the oppressive legalism of the religious establishment, his rejection of the mythology that made sin and suffering balance out ("His blindness has nothing to do with his sins or his parents' sins."—John 9:3, T.E.V.), and his impartation of forgiveness with all its attendant healing and relief will do for a start. His assault on the legal tradition challenged values, and went even further to challenge the patterns of social organization, role definitions, the distribution of prestige and authority. As Thomas Ogletree stresses in this connection, Jesus questioned the very legitimacy of the roles of the Pharisees and Sadducees.[6] He seems to have seen an oppression in the Jewish community which was more crucial for challenge than even the tyranny of Rome—perhaps because its bondage was subtler or rendered more odious by its perversion of the religious tradition it represented. His cross became an energizing power of the powerless through the Easter miracle.

In the case of the place of women, he did not make a direct attack on the patriarchal assumptions of his Jewish heritage, just as he did not initiate an abolitionist program on the slavery issue. In both cases, though, he said and did things which had implications for liberation. Somehow, even Paul, whose attitudes concerning women are Exhibit A for feminist attacks on the Christian tradition, got the idea that "There is no such thing as Jew and Greek, slave and freeman, male and female; for you are all one person in Christ Jesus" (Galatians 3:28, N.E.B.). For some reason women were among Jesus' most devoted followers—last to leave Golgotha, first to reach the tomb (although the tradition belittles their importance as witnesses to the Resurrection). Certainly Jesus' general prohibition of divorce was a boost for women's equality in a time when there were virtually no grounds for divorce for women, but a man who chose his rabbinic authority carefully could shed a wife over a burnt meal or an unkind word.

Dorothy Sayers has to rely heavily on assumption in the words which follow, but they are still worth including in our reflections on the implications of Jesus' ministry for women's liberation:

> Perhaps it is no wonder that the women were first at the Cradle and last at the Cross. They had never known a man like this Man—there never has been such another. A prophet and teacher who never nagged at them, never flattered or coaxed or patronised; who never made arch jokes about them, never treated them either as "The women, God help us!" or "The ladies, God bless them!"; who rebuked without querulousness and praised

without condescension; who took their questions and arguments seriously; who never mapped out their sphere for them, never urged them to be feminine or jeered at them for being female; who had no axe to grind and no uneasy male dignity to defend; who took them as he found them, and was completely unself-conscious. There is no act, no sermon, no parable in the whole Gospel that borrows its pungency from female perversity; nobody could possibly guess from the words and deeds of Jesus that there was anything "funny" about woman's nature.[7]

It goes almost without saying that the church which has followed Jesus, however haltingly, has staggered as badly or worse on the equality of women as it has on other kinds of human liberation. It should still be apparent, however, that liberation is what Christianity is supposedly all about.

At least since Harvey Cox renovated secular man's notion of exorcism in *The Secular City,* concern for shattering the shackles of suprapersonal systems, institutions, ideologies, etc., has come into its own. On many sides strides toward freedom from whatever enslaves man are being drawn into the core of the meaning of the Christian message. It is urged that the church must align itself not with the conservatism of interests vested in the status quo but with those forces for change which reverse processes of dehumanization and shake structures of stultification and exploitation. Liberation means the dispelling of myths which translate into legitimations for leaving people in poverty, for continuing the ugly destructiveness and imperialism which accompany the attempts of U.S. foreign policy to impose its *Pax Americana* on the world, and for continuing to make of women the second sex. The Miss America mythology, the southern womanhood mythology, the motherhood mythology, the Playboy mythology, and many other life-shaping views of the feminine ideal and of woman's nature, place, and proper role have been demonic deniers of freedom of choice and personal fulfillment to those who have lived the myths or rather let the myths live them. Captivity to the beauty parlor syndrome, which roots in anxiety about losing glamour when one serves no other needed function, does pale in comparison to the bondage of ghetto existence, but it is still a demonic kind of bondage.

When myths begin to deny access to careers because of a law school admissions policy or because of the lowered horizons of a girl who figures she should be a nurse when she could be a doctor, then their sinister qualities become clearer. When sex appeal is constantly portrayed as woman's sole bargaining power for getting the best break she can in life, whether in marriage or otherwise, the need for liberation from such an "ahead via bed" perspective ought to be obvious. When acting like a woman becomes contrived helplessness and abandoned intellectual toughness and vacuous decorativeness, then exorcism is clearly called for. The church should have a stake in the shattering of myths which foreclose freedom by making people fit roles which are rigidly defined and closing doors which might have led to personal fulfillment and to greater service to others.

The continuing debate over whether the church should simply aim at liberating individual souls or implement its preaching of deliverance to captives by social action to change laws, structures, and public policies has hopefully been softened by the evidence that massive revivals and multiple sermons on brotherhood didn't produce many steps toward racial justice that were visible to the naked eye until some direct and concerted political pressure was used. It should go without saying that liberating people has political dimensions, even if saints have proclaimed themselves free while shackled and imprisoned. It should also be apparent that changing laws and public policies can do only so much unless there is a change in the attitudes of the victims about themselves and of the victimizers about the victims. Both black and women's movements have shown that lobbying, boycotting, and other political action need to go on simultaneously with consciousness raising. Neither of them is naive enough to buy Charles Reich's assertion that a conversion of everyone to Consciousness III would automatically pull the rug from under all the systemic evils of an economic or political sort and that until then political action is irrelevant. The church shouldn't be, either. Liberation is personal and political; neither is complete without the other and each contributes to the other.

Of course, all "liberation" is not baptized because the same word is used by terrorists, anarchists, and self-indulgers (not self-actualizers) as well as by social activists and interpersonal-relations buffs whose means are more restrained, whose answers are less nihilistic, and who are more humanistic than libertine. Jesus was a revolutionary, but his revolution was not Barrabas' zealot-brand revolution. The gospel then affords not just an endorsement of people's desires for liberation but also a critique of the paths they choose and the strategies they employ.

A Christian standpoint then should make us liberation-minded. It should also make one aware that liberationists of whatever variety are sinners, just as the perpetrators of the enslaving systems, myths, and restrictions are. For instance, we are justly judged by much of what the women's liberationists say but not by all they say. The fact that I do not know the trouble they have seen does not mean that my only responses to an assertion of humanity I strongly support must be to grovel in my guilt and ask no questions. Sources of feminine stultification may be both partly unveiled and partly obscured by an economic analysis of male domination. Most marriages may well deserve the attacks of the feminists, but it just may be too simple to insist that the elimination of the institution of marriage along with a capitalistic economy will bring in the women's lib equivalent of the Kingdom of God. When women say they will go anywhere and campaign for any women running for office, I have to take exception. There's a difference between a predisposition in someone's favor if he's black or she's a woman and voting a straight sexual or racial ticket no matter what. The critical eye, then, will be peeled for what does indeed enslave women and for what can free them, but it need not always see eye to eye with the most strident and absolutistic of the feminist forces. The trick is to cooperate in the movement toward greater freedom of choice and sharing of power by women and yet keep one's critical capacities. These capacities need to be retained or developed not as a defense against the trauma of personal and societal change, but as a defense against the kind of guilty groveling that characterizes the variety of white liberals who have loved the verbal flagellations of all and sundry blacks and taken full blame for every racial crime in the world. They need also to be retained as a defense against the absolutism which claims that women can't settle for less than "total annihilation of a system which systematically destroys half its people."[8]

The charge of many feminists against Christianity has been the Marxist one that it has been in the main an opiate for women rather than a liberator of them. Like psychotherapy and marriage, religion is viewed as a diffuser of woman's discontent, an individualizer of her problems, and a subordinator of her to another set of "father figures." Backed by a patriarchal Old Testament which views women as property and a New Testament which preaches submission to husband, the church, it seems, has perpetrated second-class citizenship for women and offered them not the realization of their being neither Jew nor Greek, bond nor free, male nor female in Christ (Galatians 3:28), but the hope of a better home in heaven where they would be just like men (Freud would love that). Black Christians sang for years about having equality, freedom, and shoes "by and by," too.

There have been St. Theresas along the way who experienced a large measure of personal liberation, but virgin and witch (pedestal and stake) mentalities have been more dominant. Just as there was abolitionist and suffragette support in the churches of the nineteenth century, there has been civil rights support and movement toward women's ordination and fuller participation in our time; but the scales tilt heavily toward defense of the status quo in the churches. The religion of comfort and consolation has been coupled with genuine opportunities for service and a degree of personal fulfillment if a woman is satisfied with a subordinate position which enjoys no formal access to positions of leadership except in adjunct organizations or in separate orders.

Tokens and Troublemakers

There are still other transferable items from the church's encounter with black power and issues of racial justice which are suggestive for appropriate response to the rising expectations and demands of women. One is that "tokenism won't get it." A "window-dressing woman," whether on the Supreme Court or on the session of the First Presbyterian Church of Somewhere, is worse than nothing if her placement occasions a cessation of efforts to draw women into the mainstream of things and if it only whets appetites that will go hungry. It's nice that Mrs. Indira Gandhi and Senator Margaret Chase Smith have made it big politically, but the success of a few can serve to accentuate the deprivation or lack of opportunity of the many.

One of the findings of analysts of riots and other forms of racial unrest is that those living on the edges of ghettos who saw how the better-off lived were more frustrated, discontented, hostile, and volatile than those in the central "prison." And also, those who had had a fair amount of education and had had hope for material career advancement kindled were more apt to riot than those with little or no education, little or no hope for any employment or better employment or improved standard of living. The intensely dissatisfied were those who had been prepared for or exposed to something better and then been denied it. We should not be surprised then that the most active women's liberationists tend to come from college-educated, middle-class, and working women. The "after B.A. blues" set in when women are educated along with men and then run into the post-commencement expectation that they retire to the hearth, become the wife of ———— and mother of ————, and put their educations in mothballs at best or in the wastebasket at worst. In the work world they suddenly realize that they are not likely to get "men's" positions and opportunities, and that they are probably going to do more dirty work for less money than their male "equals." Suddenly it dawns on them that they had naively believed they were just as able as anyone else and just as free. Now they are expected to retire to traditional niches which satisfied their grandmothers and maybe even their mothers, but not them. Many have been deciding they aren't going to settle for less than a larger life and have gotten "uppity."

Ironically enough, the deepest disillusionment came to women in the civil rights movement and in various radical political movements who thought they were within sight of victory for themselves as well as for blacks, students, etc. Then Stokely Carmichael announced that "the only position for women in S.N.C.C. is prone."[9] It became obvious that there wouldn't be any women presidents of S.D.S. chapters and that women were once again being relegated to legwork, paper work, and dirty work while the men ran the show. Some sisters decided they weren't going to "take it lying down." Robin Morgan says:

> Goodbye to the illusion of strength when you run hand in hand with your oppressors; goodbye to the dream that being in the leadership collective will get you anything but gonorrhea.[10]

The liberators were thus discovered to be enslavers when it comes to women, and the world began to find out politically that hell would have to go some to have fury like at least some scorned women.

Being told "You've come a long way, baby" doesn't get it when people want freedom now and not glacial progress toward the redress of wrongs. It is true that girl babies are no longer left to die of exposure, that women are no longer considered property, that they can own property, that it is no longer argued very widely whether they should receive college educations, that they have the vote, and that they even have their own cigarette and the possibility of being offered a cigarillo. If they weren't going to get the whole package, though, it would have been better not to start

the process. How're you going to keep them barefoot and pregnant once they've read Kate Millett and Germaine Greer?

Those who said "I knew we shouldn't have given them the
vote" had a point. A little freedom, a little hope, a little progress
are dangerous things unless men really are going to follow through
and open the way for full liberation of women.

Who Can Help Whom?

Still another parallel which is useful in responding creatively
to women's liberation has to do with who can help whom and
how. After the legal barriers have been removed and certain rights
have been assured *de jure* (and at this writing we are hopefully
on the way to ratification of an amendment on that score for
women), there comes the much slower, more painstaking process
of getting the "in" group or person to think differently about
itself.

Just as some black leaders have asserted that white sympa-
thizers would do well to devote their efforts to getting white
attitudes in line rather than running the civil rights organizations,
so women can now maintain that the "problem" is largely the
man's problem and that straightening out the male segment of
society would be all men can do to destroy sexual servitude. The
rest women must do themselves. Contemporary writers on white
racism such as George Colman and Robert Terry of the Detroit
Industrial Mission have pointed out that there is no such thing
as a passive anti-racist. One may be an active racist (bigot) or a
passive racist (conformist) or an active anti-racist, but he cannot
be a passive anti-racist. To be passive is to continue to live with
the problem—the white problem—and thus to perpetuate the
"denial of justice [defined in terms of self-determination, respect,
openness, and pluralism] to people of color by individuals, groups,
institutions, and cultures and the rationalization of such behavior
by attributing inferior characteristics to those denied justice."[11]
True anti-racism seeks to make whites aware of their problem and

to be active in turning back a tide with which the passive merely ride. By this definition blacks couldn't be racist if they wanted to be, and it's beside the point to attack black separatism. Similarly one can say that men had better concentrate on setting themselves straight and that keeping their gears in neutral keeps them in the sexist category only. We are all part of the problem. Those who are actively anti-sexist are also part of the solution.

Despite location of the problem in white and male attitudes, black leaders and feminists have known that there was a problem with their own attitudes—in particular the problem of their continuing to look at themselves as inferior and to adapt themselves to the very stereotypes which shackle them. Therefore, the black leadership seeks to build black consciousness and black pride, and the feminist forerunners have likewise focused much effort on building women's awareness of their oppression and faith in their worth and equality, if not superiority. Small group consciousness-raising sessions for women are a big part of most women's liberation programs for change. Not surprisingly this thrust sometimes carries to the extreme of urging sexual separatism and virtual guerrilla warfare. Buyers of the "hate bit" appear to be few among women, but the heightened female consciousness is a growing reality.

"Broad Is Beautiful"

One thing that the black movement for pride and power might have taught women better than it has is the implications of the slogan "Black is beautiful." Although the slogan "Bitch is beautiful" has been sounded in the "Bitch Manifesto," its definition of bitchiness is such an obvious opposite of the traditional stereotypes of femininity that one is reminded of political ideologies that are totally dictated by an anti-stance. In part, its authoress, Joreen, writes:

> Bitches have some or all of the following characteristics.
> 1) *Personality*. Bitches are aggressive, assertive, domineer-

ing, overbearing, strong-minded, spiteful, hostile, direct, blunt, candid, obnoxious, thick-skinned, hard-headed, vicious, dogmatic, competent, competitive, pushy, loud-mouthed, independent, stubborn, demanding, manipulative, egoistic, driven, achieving, overwhelming, threatening, scary, ambitious, tough, brassy, masculine, boisterous, and turbulent. Among other things. A Bitch occupies a lot of psychological space. You always know she is around. A Bitch takes shit from no one. You may not like her, but you cannot ignore her.

2) *Physical.* Bitches are big, tall, strong, large, loud, brash, harsh, awkward, clumsy, sprawling, strident, ugly. Bitches move their bodies freely rather than restrain, refine, and confine their motions in the proper feminine manner. They clomp up stairs, stride when they walk and don't worry about where they put their legs when they sit. They have loud voices and often use them. Bitches are not pretty.[12]

In the tradition of the defender of Elizabeth Taylor who said, "Anyone who divorces Eddie Fisher can't be all bad," the paranoiac anticommunist, for instance, knows only that he's against it if the Russians or Cubans or Chinese are for it and if it can be given the label "socialistic." Like the child who in his rebellion is still dominated by his parents because he is compelled to diametrically oppose them on every issue, decision, and act, a pack of "bitches" and "witches" (their own designation) can be observed that is in fact still enslaved by masculine and feminine stereotypes. A new stereotype is produced by a knee-jerk rejection of the traditional. Instead of attempting to shake off the dehumanizing facets of both "masculine" models and "feminine" models and to discover a new sense of pride and identity as women, these people try to reject everything that has supposedly been deemed "natural" to women or socially prescribed for them, or they actually adopt stereotypes of maleness as the definition of true personhood and thus imitate the ugliness of their oppressors.

My own suggestion in an earlier article of the slogan "Broad is beautiful" for the emerging female consciousness was well intended, but since "broad" is viewed by many women as a derisive male label which implies mindless sexuality, another option is needed. The important thing is that without the ability to accept and glory in one's being a woman one remains chained to the negative view of one's sex that is the root of the thralldom and the bitterness in the first place. One also remains committed to male (compare white) ideals which need to be called into serious question. The feminist match for an "Oreo" (black on the outside but white inside) is the woman who has completely internalized a male mentality though she must still exist in a female physique. Being male is okay, being female isn't.

The Realities of Power

Another ethically significant lesson to be learned from the political struggles of the black community is that the powerful rarely if ever abdicate their advantageous positions out of the goodness of their hearts. Friendly discussions and helpful suggestions may help with some male members of the power structure, but voting power and publicity pressure are usually the softest language to which the "in's" will listen. Some might even theorize that the extreme unlikelihood of widespread outbreaks of female violence will mean continued failure of many to take women's protests seriously. However, the surprising success of George McGovern's coming from nowhere to nomination for President has been credited to the "nylon revolution" by noted analyst of president-making Theodore White. When it dawns on the rest of the country what a difference a grass-roots army of women organizers made, they will begin to get some respect—maybe even some fear. If women really begin to identify with all their sisters and act together, who knows what such tactics as block voting, lobbying, public dramatization of issues, and the formation of the National Women's Political Caucus might do to influence public policy as it affects woman's situation in society.

It is a cinch that many of the entries women seek will not open without some pushing on the door and that they must walk in rather than expect to be carried across the threshold. Being coddled or carried on a silver platter does not liberate, even if men were eager to give up their dominant position in society. And unless the human race evolves to a transcendence of self-interest which has never been seen before, a note in the suggestion box is not going to make the boss trade places with his secretary.

The Relevance of Principle

A final transfer which the Christian ethicist can fruitfully make from the black experience to woman's experience is in the realm of relevant principles. If one starts from certain theological convictions or ethical orientations which affirm that each person is to be valued in his or her uniqueness, that the human family should be an inclusive and not an exclusive fellowship, and that equitable treatment and the advancement of freedom for self-fulfillment are normative, one arrives at certain policy directives which apply alike to women and to blacks. A clear mandate would be that of equal opportunity.[13] If there never is an equal number of truck drivers, engineers, lawyers, and secretaries among men and women, that need cause no concern provided the way is genuinely open for blacks and women to prepare for and do these jobs which they personally desire and are able to handle. Along with equal opportunity as a demand of justice should go full participation by women in the decisions which shape their destinies.

If equal opportunity is a mandate of distributive justice or equity, "affirmative action" should be an expression of compensatory justice for those who have been wronged. Figuring up the proper monetary return on all women's labors in the home and the proper compensation for their sub-male pay for equal work would be impossible even if the payers and the payees were agreeable and agreed on the amount. (Do husbands owe wives an hourly wage for their work in the home which enables the husband to earn outside the home and to bring bacon home to wife and children?) However, just as it is not enough for a formerly all-white college or corporation simply to announce that it will now accept qualified black students or employees, the simple dropping of quotas or restrictions on women does nothing to make up for the past. The inequities and discriminations of the past cannot be undone or made up in most cases, but "affirmative action" involves actively seeking out persons from the mistreated group for employment, enrollment, and promotion above job ceilings. It's time extra efforts were made to get women into graduate programs, supervisory positions, elective offices, and other areas where they have met sexual detours if not roadblocks in the past. Setting quotas for women's representation on delegate slates to Democratic conventions in 1972 seemed artificial and unnecessary to some and illegal to at least one federal judge, but there was compensatory justice and affirmative action in it. Various "women's studies" courses in colleges and universities, like black studies courses, are another example.

The principles of distributive and compensatory justice are just two of the derivative generalizations about social justice for women which are transferable from the social ethics of black liberation. If the church has come, however belatedly, to the implementation of these and other principles for blacks, she can hardly rationalize the exclusion of women from the directives to social policy which are implied by the Christian faith.

Differing Conditions of Servitude

The elaboration of the analogies between the victimization and the liberation of black people and of female people could be stretched considerably further. However, the analogy, like any analogy, can be fruitfully pushed only so far. As the fellow said, "Generalizations ain't worth a damn—including this one."

Germaine Greer calls the comparison "misleading,"[14] and some are even calling a halt in the use of it. Catharine Stimpson, for instance, believes that "women's liberation would be much stronger, much more honest, ultimately more secure if it stopped comparing white women to blacks so freely." Despite the dividends women are collecting from the seared consciences and heightened sensitivities which the civil rights and black power movements have occasioned, Stimpson sees problems. The women need to make their case stand on its own rather than remain in a fellow-traveling relationship. Yoking the two movements limits protest to the American scene, when sexism is a planetary problem. It lumps blacks and white women as "amorphous, classless, blobby masses."[15] It evades white women's racism and black men's sexism. It neglects the fact that many black women see white women as overprivileged possessors of a lot they want and that black men see white women as competitors for jobs.

The two movements are largely separable under Norman Faramelli's pre-affluent (poor and black) and post-affluent (youth and women) categories.[16] Getting to stay home with her children might be liberation for many underemployed and underpaid black mothers. Class must be considered along with sex and caste. Again, both in terms of ingroup fears and in terms of outgroup purposes, violence and the threat of violence is not really a factor in the women's liberation movement. As Stimpson says, "A woman, carrying a gun, despite the fact that women can and do shoot, is politically ineffective in America. Our culture finds it bizarre, and I, for one, find it regressive."[17] One plank of most women's liberation platforms is a repudiation of violence as a means of political bargaining and of undermining and destroying the sexist system. Violence is out, just as top-dog–bottom-dog power relations are. Merely to put women in the driver's seat would not be enough. The car needs to be traded in. These women want egalitarianism, but not through the old *machismo* methods or at the expense of men's liberation. Says Germaine Greer:

> Wars cannot be *won*, as any Englishman ruefully contrasting his postwar fortunes with those of guilty Nazi Europe is confusedly aware. Women who adopt the attitudes of war in their search for

liberation condemn themselves to acting out the last perversion of
dehumanized manhood, which has only one foreseeable outcome,
the specifically masculine end of suicide.

It is slavery to rely on guile and dissimulation, but it is no revolution to let the evil system choose the weapons for the conflict
when those means themselves are part of the problem.[18]

The causes need to be distinguished, and the previous conditions of the two groups should not be equated. If you ask black
men and white women whose shoes each would have preferred to
wear, in terms of educational opportunity, political equality, special privileges, and material well-being in this country, in 1950 or
even in 1960 and maybe even in 1970, the women's shoes would
probably get the decision by a landslide vote. They had their
Jackie Robinsons long before the Dodgers took on more color in
Brooklyn. Black women have, of course, had double trouble all the
way along.

White women can argue now that some black men and even
black women are getting breaks just because they're black in the
areas of jobs, college scholarships, etc., but that government agencies are not yet holding women's quotas up to employers. They
can also argue that even though the oppression of blacks has been
more obvious and more physically cruel for the most part, the
subjugation of women is more ancient, more basic, subtler, more
stubborn, in the final analysis. Betty Roszak speaks of male society's disparagement of women as having "all the force of an unconscious conspiracy" which is "even more subtle than the racist and
colonial oppressions to which it is closely allied, because it is
softened and hidden by the silken padding of eroticism."[19]

Still another argument is that women regardless of race have
been more disadvantaged than men, including nonwhite men. In
1969, for instance, white women earned $2,600 less than white
men and $1,500 less than nonwhite men, while nonwhite women
earned $3,800 less than white men, $1,900 less than nonwhite
men, and $1,200 less than white women.[20] The catch is that

despite the obvious injustice revealed by the figures, women have shared the larger income of men to a great extent. Marriage, despite its evils, has afforded a social elevator for white women that blacks have not had.[21]

Women's time of victimization has often not been a time of impoverishment materially, and political and educational opportunities which have come lately, if at all, to blacks have belonged to women for as long as any of today's feminists can remember. This does not mean, however, that human alienation is not most fundamentally expressed in the relations between the sexes and that the overcoming of alienation must not ultimately get to this most fundamental level if it is to be genuine.

The overall societal influence of women has also far exceeded that of blacks. The means may have been "feminine wiles" or sexual bribery or working on "him" through the children or hurt looks or subtle suggestions. Certainly the formal authority has been largely absent, but the power has been considerable. The Arkansas pastor of a Presbyterian church who complained in 1962 that the Holy Spirit could not lead his session (all men in those days) until the members had gone home and talked with their wives was not joking, and the case of Daniel Ellsberg and the "Pentagon Papers" is only one instance of a wife's influence on shapers of public policy. I won't claim that no woman has ever influenced a man toward a more hawkish stance, but some of Ellsberg's public statements would imply that more influence by women would counteract rather than confirm the Pentagon mentality.

An article by former Senator Paul Douglas entitled "Three Saints in Politics" deals with the conscientious dedication and the amazing integrity of (1) Jerry Voorhis, ten years a congressman from California before his victimization by a nasty smear campaign, which brought his loss to Richard Nixon; (2) Frank Graham, beloved president of the University of North Carolina and short-time U.S. senator who suffered defeat in a racist campaign, and (3) Herbert Lehman, senator from New York and reformer of the Democratic Party. It was striking that in each case some passing reference by Douglas to the wives of the three men told the careful reader that the political convictions and efforts of these three remarkable men were the products of a partnership of concern and conscience with their mates.[22]

The old saw about rocking the cradle and swaying the nation points to one pressure point of skirt power, and the frequent absence of the father's role in the family would suggest that women's shaping of the young has grown steadily—at least in proportion to male adult influences. Kenneth Keniston's *Young Radicals* provides one analysis of this phenomenon.

However, there are other reasons why women's influence has exceeded that of the usual oppressed minority. For one thing, women are a majority, not a minority. The sheer dent of numbers has doubtless had some impact. For another, as Helen Mayer Hacker suggests, women are more important to the dominant group than are blacks.[23] A greater ambivalence marks the male-female relationship than the black-white one. Attraction and need wield at least as much impact as contempt and desire for distance and independence. This ambivalence is illustrated in the female stereotypes which include laudable and revered and socially valuable characteristics as well as less desirable qualities. Women have been both vilified (the Witch or Bitch) and deified (the Goddess), unlike blacks (except for a few "noble savage" instances).[24] Further, there is only one other sex which stands in biological juxtaposition to men, while there are plural ethnic and racial minorities.

It is also the contrasting case that women are scattered (or infiltrated?) throughout a society rather than ghettoized. They are a class within each class. Politically this latter fact has been a curse and a blessing. Among the blessings has been something of an "insider" status, even though men often talked business and politics in the other room. Women have profited from their men's gains and often used them in ways which influenced the economy, promoted the arts, and aided the needy. Supposedly some husbands and wives have genuinely loved each other, and supposedly genuine love does produce some actual sharing and some mutual effects of one partner on the other. I seriously doubt that any genuinely loved wife has ever felt like nothing more than a slave or believed that all marriages are part of a deliberate political strategy of men to make and keep women cheap, easily controllable domestic and commercial serfs, breeders, and child-tenders. Betty Roszak's labeling of the institution of marriage as "an economic bargain glossed over by misty sentimentalizing" is another of those famous generalizations, for what it's worth.[25]

The curse of women's diffusion has been that the solidarity, the awareness of oppression, and the ready-made power base which are the by-products of ghetto living have been lost to the scattered women, who were apt to think of their problems as narrowly personal rather than pervasively social and who had enjoyed the benefits of the system enough to be "bought up." Black solidarity was there to be mobilized; "Sisterhood" was harder to come by. The feminists who are most vocal about deliberate political subjugation on the part of men see in all this a male strategy to keep women at home with the dishes, the children, and other women's activities, and out of men's hair and out of trouble. Like some fertilizers, it seems women could keep the crop growing if they were scattered and kept in their several places, whereas a concentration of them might raise a stink. "Divide and conquer" then is supposedly part of the plan of attack in the battle of the sexes.

The Personal and the Political

All of these considerations raise important questions about the relation between interpersonal ethics and political ethics. In the racial arena we know only too well that claims about personal love between masters and slaves and later between a black domestic employee and the family obscured issues of equality and justice with paternalistic handouts and treatment as children. Ethicists reminded us that love was at least justice, that loving someone or some group meant treating them as equals and demanding justice for them. Some of the language of liberationists would suggest that men's "love" for women is reducible to the same opposition to justice, and needs to have "in their place" attached. My own feeling is that despite my hatred for the flagrant injustices which were and are permitted to continue in the presence of personal love for "our Nigrahs," there has often been real mutual love between blacks and whites, though not to the exclusion of more resentment than we "honkies" have usually realized. Even more do I feel that love between men and women has often been genuine and mutual despite the injustices of a set of conventions and cultural attitudes which for a long time both sides largely took for granted. I'm not as ready as Germaine Greer to deny that love between superiors and inferiors is impossible,[26] even if domination is wrong. Now that the deceptive veneer has come unglued and some of the rottenness and ugliness of what had been hidden from general view is out in the open, love, of course, has no excuse for being blind.

There is a question of the interpersonal and the political which has nothing to do with paternalism's peace with injustice. Confronted with ethical decision-making in situations involving sexual behavior on dates, treatment of an employee in need, or keeping a promise to a friend, in contrast to situations involving boycotts, collective bargaining, suburban zoning ordinances, or test-ban treaties, some types of moral reflection have put these issues in two virtually distinct categories. On the one side are the person-to-person relationships, which should be directed by love which is self-sacrificing, nonviolent, and unconditional. On the other are the power confrontations between institutions, interest groups, parties, nations, etc., in which a balance of power and some approximation of justice are the best that can be expected realistically. Personal, I-to-thou ethics then are a horse of a quite different color from political, we-to-them or it-to-it ethics. Love and power are then deemed antithetical, and the ideal and the necessary are given their near-separate compartments.

The fact is that a continuum provides a better way of sorting out these matters than compartments. The degree of complexity, the forms of pressure, and levels of trust vary greatly when one moves from the moral dimensions of a congressional decision about whether to continue military aid to Greek and Pakistani regimes which are more than tinged with totalitarianism to the dilemma of how best to help two friends who are contemplating divorce. The differences are best understood, however, as matters of degree rather than kind if we are not to succumb to moral schizophrenia.

In the specific area of relations between the sexes and life in the family, we kid ourselves if we think we are in the realm of the apolitical. Bedfellows make strange politics, but they do make them and always will. Anyone who doesn't think a marriage or a family is a political unit has not been a very aware part of either. The exercise of power and the confrontation of one interest by another, necessitating compromise, are part of all human relationships, and the women's liberationists have done us the service of exploding the romanticism which fails to understand sexual relations in political and economic terms and to discern the social, institutional dimensions of each individual marriage. However, some of the most ideological statements and manifestos have been reductionistically political-economic and institutional. The interpersonal has been forgotten. The possibilities of love and power riding together in relationships and of the I-thou transcending the I-it are belittled, if not negated, in the preoccupation with group exploitation.

On the other side of the personal-political split, many women have seethed about their own predicaments, but, under the assumption that it was merely a personal matter, have failed to see the social traditions, institutions, laws, and attitudes which have taken their toll on all women and will not waver before the single objections or nonconformities of isolated women. Psychotherapy and pietistic religion, two popular refuges of "maladjusted" women, have often reinforced the assumption that "the problem" is each woman's personal one. Supposedly, if a woman can get straightened out personally, things will work out. The venom in the attacks of some women liberationists against psychotherapists, ministers, priests, and marriage counselors is due to the fact that men in most cases (or women who have been taken in by the sexist mentality) are daring to locate the malaise in individuals when it should be considered a sign of health for women to be unhappy in a sick society. Kathy Mulherin, in an article she and Jennifer Gardner did called "Growing Up a Woman," recalls a quiet woman in her fifties who, unable to talk with her husband, had seethed inwardly but assumed her problems were personal. Then she heard about the widespread expectations that a single girl should move in with a guy, keep house, maybe even support him, and then be left to pay the rent when he decides to split. At that point she began to talk of her daughter and said, "Maybe your movement could do something for her."[27]

In *Sexual Politics*, Kate Millett calls for an end to sexual politics. She understandably does that because for her politics refers to the domination of one group by another. She has a near-conspiratorial view of sexual politics as now practiced and cannot envision any "political" interaction which would not aim at or eventuate in a domination situation. A counteractive style is seen in the organizational structure of the magazine *Ms.* and of women's liberation groups which eschew hierarchy, officers, monopolization of functions, for the sake of shared authority, participatory democracy, rotating responsibilities, and maximum development of each person. Talking permits are even rationed to prevent monopolization of discussions by the charismatic and super-articulate.

If we can accept Herbert Richardson's contentions in *Nun, Witch, Playmate* concerning the democratizing effects of the development of romantic love on the family and society at large, we can greatly qualify Millett's anti-politics. If the democratic family has flowered from romantic roots, why cannot the politics of democracy—of give and take, of conflict and compromise, of checks and balances—be retained when men and women get liberated from a hierarchial model of the family?

Millett, of course, wants the end of the institution of marriage (which for her means patriarchal monogamy) and with it the politics of the sexes. Greer similarly insists that women who seek liberation must refuse to marry and that love can exist outside of marriage.[28] Beyond that, one wonders what the following quotations from Ms. Greer's book tell us about her dim view of marriage and the family.

> My father had decided fairly early on that life at home was pretty unbearable; and he lived more and more of it at his club, only coming home to sleep.
>
> Not all women are as desperate as my mother was when she used to mutter to me that my father was a "senile old goat."
>
> Once my mother knelt on my small brother's chest and beat his face with her fists in front of my father and was threatened with violent retaliation, the only instance of my father's rising to her bait that I can recall. My brother was three years old at the time.
>
> I can recall being beaten for giving away all my toys when I was about four.[29]

The first problem with many liberationists' aversion to marriage is that marriage is not about to wither away, despite the increasing number of alternatives that are appearing and gaining followers. Many of these, I hasten to add, are "marriage" by some other name. The second is that man is a political animal and that even the communes and other options to monogamy have their politics. Life can proceed with some predictability and stability only as people make promises, identify with various bodies politic, and interact with each other against the background of more or less formal institutional centers.

As marriages have become more democratic, they have had a better chance to educate both partners in the grinds and grates of social life. If faithful love undergirds the marital body politic, there can be some head knocking (figuratively speaking), some confrontations, and some hard learning in an atmosphere where threat is minimized. People who love each other and have made a permanent commitment to function in a body politic with each other have a far better chance for growing up to mature concern for others' welfare than do people in a relationship that is "of the moment" and will by prior mutual understanding be terminated at individual whim. By advocating sexual politics, I am not excusing barter-with-the-bed privileges but only recognizing that the bed may be the best context for exerting influence on the other, not because "favors" are withheld if the other does not shape up but because "favors" continue even when there is conflict and misunderstanding. Knowledge that you have let down someone you love has its own pressures, too.

The introduction of children into a marriage of course heightens the political character of the institution of marriage. Attempts to line up children on the side of one of the parents against the other and grim endurances of a marriage "for the children's sake" are sick examples of children's influences on a marriage. However, children do often prevent marriages from becoming as ingrown or as capricious as they might otherwise be. The couples who have agreed that the first person to mention divorce gets custody of the children have their own way of affirming that you just don't walk out of marriage any day you feel like it and leave entanglements behind.

As children grow up in a family where the authority is truly shared and power is exercised within the context of love, they have a chance to become schooled in at least some of the political realities of the larger body politic. On the other hand, if either parent dominates, they may come to see love in doormat terms and power in domination terms and thus separate the two. If the children are allowed to dominate, then they are headed for speedy disillusionment with the larger institutional realities of society which do not respond immediately to their slightest wish. They are perhaps also headed toward an anarchic and even violent repudiation of the entire system under the utopian assumption that society could function like the totally permissive homes they come from.

The ability of love to transcend the limitations of institutional interaction and even to transform the institutions could shed some important light on the matter of allies and adversaries of the women's liberation movement. Not many women could agree with Valerie Solanas that men should be exterminated. Ti-Grace Atkinson of the Feminists has more support in her call for an end to sex with "the enemy," but it is hardly formidable. There is plenty of sentiment, however, which makes men "the enemy." If the feminist perspective should insist on making men only the adversary, then the possibility of husbands and wives fighting together the objectionable injustices to women in the conventional scheme of things is precluded. On the other hand, if more men come to believe that they too need liberation from sexist stereotypes, which hem them in as well as women, it will be possible for men and women to join forces against what a system they have not personally created is doing to them both. Hostility is thus turned away from each other to laws, conventions, and myths which are dehumanizing both men and women. If men can be helped to see their own needs for liberation, then the "we" versus "them" attitude which results from pitting the sexes against each other can be overcome.

Integration Versus Separation

In the civil rights movement, integration became suspect because it meant blending into the white scheme of things on the white society's terms. The question of integration as an ultimate goal came to be bracketed if not discarded because black identity, dignity, and power had to come first to enable a joining of equals if there was to be any joining at all. As long as equality and self-determination and material well-being can be achieved, the full integration of society has become a low priority for many blacks if not a thing to be avoided. Black pastors have raised serious questions about church unions which might break up black churches. The breakup of black residential communities through urban renewal and other programs has long been under fire, and community control of public schools has become a goal on which black and white anti-busers could at times agree. A minority could lose its identity and get absorbed.

Given these drawbacks, which blacks have identified with integration understood as assimilation, Judith Benninger Brown asserts that marriage does to women just what integration does to blacks. She calls marriage "the atomization of a sex so as to render it politically powerless."[30]

The woman's situation is, however, not quite the same. She may feel that she has been swallowed up despite her majority in numbers and that she needs to assert some independence to keep from being taken for granted and taken in. The strident assertions that women don't need men, whether they are couched in sexual terms about the myth of the vaginal orgasm or in social and political terms of sexual separatism or sexual warfare, just don't convince me. I can imagine how it must make the blood of a women's liberationist boil when males respond to her impassioned attacks with knowing smiles and whispered diagnoses to the effect that "she just needs a man." I also understand the ire which accompanies reactions to male or female suggestions that the single person can't really be living a full life since the key to wedlock opens the door to happiness. (Why, though, must the only alternative make it the door to prison?) What is hard to buy is any contention that "total integration" (not to be understood as female assimilation in a male-dominated society) is not a top-priority item for men and women alike.

Alice Rossi discusses three models for the relation of a minority group in society.[31] The first is the pluralist model, which seems dominant in black circles now and which retains and values racial, religious, and ethnic differences in a heterogeneous society. The second is the assimilation model, which amounts to an absorption and which is another name for what "integration" came to mean for blacks and what militant feminists are asserting has happened to women. The hybrid model is the third. It suggests a change in both ascendant and minority groups to make a third kind of society which differs from any of its plural predecessors. This model would perhaps overdo the elimination of differences, which will be discussed in the ensuing chapter, but it underlines the transformation which both male and female roles might undergo in the marriages or non-marriages and the larger society of the future.

Increasingly one senses a trend in this hybrid direction. If there is a battle of the sexes, both sides seem to want to work it out. Men can learn to love their wives like "sisters." Some marriages are changing creatively, not just disintegrating. Fights within the family can be bitter, but there is still a difference between family quarrels and either class conflict or racial hostility. On this score Alice Rossi points out that a hard press for sex equality may create tensions in a marriage, whereas ethnic, racial, and religious conflicts may cement families by common oppressors and common objects of hatred or resentment. Rossi aptly pinpoints the inhibition of fear of conflict with their husbands which keeps women from expressing and protesting their grievances, and reminds us of the high percentage of unmarried or no-longer-married women in liberation leadership. What she overlooks is the creative possibilities in the family situation which are at least equal to the hindrances to liberation. Maybe I am naive, but women don't seem very much afraid of their husbands among our friends and acquaintances.

The message about women's liberation and the maintenance of the woman's individuality, rather than her losing her identity in husband and children, has obviously gotten to the couples I marry these days. However, marriage isn't declining in popularity among young people I know, and they think they can work it out. They are not totally sentimental, and they believe the institution of marriage is reformable and that it can be a personal covenant as well as an economic bargain. Waking up to the economics and politics of relations between the sexes should not mislead us into a denial of the possibilities of friendship and communion between an I and a Thou.

Glendy Culligan's reaction to feminist obituaries for the institution of marriage would seem to have some supporters still.

> Marriage as an institution, however, has functions beyond procreation and may not be quite ready for the scrapheap. With some exceptions, these authors seem insufficiently familiar with its desirable features, both sexual and social. "Never underestimate the power of a man" might well become a rallying cry of the opposition if extreme feminists continue to ignore biochemistry in their austere blueprints for the future. Raising children is also much more fun than they acknowledge and can be intellectually as well as emotionally rewarding. Having been a dependent wife and an independent head of household, a working and a nonworking mother, I cannot agree that any of those situations is necessarily degrading. Like the eighteenth-century houses still standing in London and Washington, marriage can be modernized to include more light and warmth without loss of its best architectural features.[32]

Judith Benninger Brown's assertion that marriage is at the mercy of more powerful institutions even if men and women are willing to transform it strikes me as an exaggeration of the economic analysis which makes marriage a necessary cog in the wheels of capitalism. And the description in the "Bitch Manifesto" of its constituency could be as politically imprudent as it is morally questionable, if marriage means personal commitment.

> Bitches seek their identity strictly through themselves and what they do. They are subjects, not objects. They may have a relationship with a person or organization, but they never *marry* anyone or anything: man, mansion, or movement.[33]

Do passing involvements or relationships carry with them the potential for personal and social change that long-term commitments with accompanying mutual trust do? Can you forsake "the System" completely and get anywhere with your goals for social change? Can you utterly destroy the system and hope to avoid all its evils with the new anti-system system? These are questions which will continue to concern us in the pages ahead.

2

Vive la Différence?

"Feminine" by Nature or Nurture?

The *bête noire* of the liberated or would-be liberated woman is the "Eternal Feminine." Germaine Greer describes this mythical ideal as follows in *The Female Eunuch:*

> The stereotype is the Eternal Feminine. She is the Sexual Object sought by all men, and by all women. She is of neither sex, for she has herself no sex at all. Her value is solely attested by the demand she excites in others. . . . She need never give positive evidence of her moral character because virtue is assumed from her loveliness, and her passivity. . . . Innocently she may drive men to madness and war. The more trouble she can cause, the more her stocks go up, for possession of her means more the more demand she excites. Nobody wants a girl whose beauty is imperceptible to all but him; and so men welcome the stereotype because it directs their taste into the most commonly recognized areas of value . . .[1]

Because of this stereotype, women (with a little *w*) are virtually rendered unreal to the extent that they are not true material expressions of some Platonic form of Woman (with a capital W). To break out of this cocooned abstraction is to deny one's womanhood. Individual females become mere instances of the Idea of "the Feminine" and to that extent become more things than people. Packaged by the lingerie and cosmetic industries, taught salesmanship from mother's knee and mother's magazines, women allow themselves to become marketable commodities and often come off as assembly-line products.

Mary Daly uses "The Pedestal Peddlars" to refer to those who support the stereotype of woman as the embodiment of some eternal feminine principle which dictates her destiny.[2] These exalters of women insist that women are as good as or better than men, but women are defined as being psychologically, not just physiologically, different from men by nature. Included in their ranks are big names in psychology (Sigmund Freud, Erich Fromm, Erik Erikson, Carl Jung, Bruno Bettleheim, and Helene Deutsch), in philosophy and theology (Teilhard de Chardin, Alfred North Whitehead, Nicholas Berdyaev, Karl Barth, and Karl Jaspers), and in literature (Claudel, Dylan Thomas, and Norman Mailer). Although these people vary greatly, it is claimed that some vestige of a "feminine mystique" persists in their view of women. The reader should be warned at this point that the writer questions tarring all these people with the same brush and that a later exposition of Jung's thought, for instance, will reveal that the similarities between his rendition of the Eternal Feminine and Germaine Greer's are scarcely visible to the naked eye.

Supporters of the Eternal Feminine see women as naturally disposed toward mothering, toward feeling, toward dependence, and toward a nonaggressive orientation, and may call any deviations from such a profile "unnatural" or "maladjusted." They might not say "Women's liberation stops at the obstetrician's door," but they would be apt to say that women's "natural" inclination is to be wives and mothers. "Anatomy is destiny" is the Freudian axiom which is often alleged to be at the heart of the Eternal Feminine position.

The environmentalists, such as Simone de Beauvoir, Betty Friedan, Karen Horney, David Riesman, Jean-Paul Sartre, Alice Rossi, Kate Millett, D. S. Bailey, Margaret Mead (although she can be quoted on both sides of the question), Sidney Callahan, and virtually the whole contingent of feminists, insist that femininity is totally learned. Nothing should be called "naturally feminine," including the deodorant spray by that name. If there are differences between men and women beyond the obvious physiological ones, they are inconsequential. These people see assertions about "equality but difference" as a subtly inferior categorization. Males are still attempting to set the limits of female functioning—perhaps more broadly than Freud's ultratraditional rendition of woman as essentially constituted by *Küche, Kirche, und Kinder,* but certainly not broadly enough to invite liberation from the motherhood myth and other restricting stereotypes.

An example of an extreme statement on the different nature of women comes from Dr. Edgar F. Berman. He has asserted that "genes are our fate and hormones our masters" and concluded that women are too unstable to be entrusted with positions of high responsibility because their monthly "raging hormonal imbalances" turn them into unstable creatures.[3] (Norman Mailer, who stands more in awe of women than in horror of their election to top leadership positions, might appear to support Berman by his inclusion in *The Prisoner of Sex* of the claim that half women's auto accidents, half women's admissions to mental hospitals, half their attempted suicides, and half the crimes of woman prisoners occur during the week of menstruation.)[4] What, Berman asked, might have happened at the Bay of Pigs if women had been in control? Dr. Estelle Ramey's perfect response is to ask what did happen and who was in control. One wonders how well Dr. Berman sleeps since a recent Gallup Poll revealed that 66 percent of Americans would vote for a qualified woman as President.

In its most extreme form environmentalism seems to draw the same conclusion that one reviewer drew after reading Kate

Millett's *Sexual Politics:* "Ignore our penises and our vaginas and we should all be the same; in a perfect world, no one would know the difference between Joe Willie Namath and Raquel Welch."[5] Beyond the obvious physiological differences, masculinity and femininity are wholly social products, and ideally the sexes would be androgynous rather than expressions of the mysterious poles of a duality.

The debate between the environmentalists and the advocates of the Eternal Feminine will perhaps never be settled, particularly since the line between nature and nurture is virtually impossible to draw with exactness. It is probably safe to say that any rigid definitions of what's "natural" will take their lumps as men and women evolve, and that any claims that culture is the sole determinant of what is called "natural" are too simple. We shall also discover that the analyses of biology and personality which underline the bisexuality of us all, or the contrasexuality in us all (the feminine in men and the masculine in women), purport to offer a third approach. This approach, which is connected especially with the thought of Carl Jung and his followers, recasts the discussion by refusing to reserve "the feminine" for women only, however they happened to have gotten "it."

Two comments on the debate can serve as guidelines for consideration of the question. The first comes from Sidney Callahan, a very able thinker and writer on the role of women from a theological perspective on the liberal wing of the Roman Catholic tradition. In conversation she admitted that she had had times of leaning in a more "mystiquey" direction but that her writings reflected her more dominant inclination to question assertions about natural differences in the male and female psyches. She asserts, for instance, that "what is fundamental in man as a *human being*—his reason and his will—is independent of physiological structure."[6] (Desmond Morris would, of course, assert that man's unique sexuality has a great influence on his reason and will.) When I raised the question about the growing realization of the close interconnection between biology and psychology, between body chemistry and character, she replied in a very friendly way, "There may be differences between men and women, but I don't want men telling me what they are." This offhand reply struck me as very important because it asked why men feel called upon to decide what women can be or ought to be or were meant to be. If there is a "feminine factor" which can be articulated as generally characteristic of women, it will be dynamic and not static, since the evolution of "human nature" goes on. And it serves no good purpose for a male-dominated society to in any way decide in advance for women what is best discovered by them in process, if indeed it exists at all. Centuries of "genetic coding" can be modified in the future.

The second comment came from a conversation with Roger Shinn, the outstanding theologian–social ethicist of Union Theological Seminary in New York. In reflecting, again in informal conversation, on a symposium on women at Union Seminary, he observed to me that the participants' views on "masculinity" and "femininity" tended to divide between psychologically-oriented persons and persons oriented more toward social action and social change. Of course, this split would, for the militant feminist, confirm the charges she has been making about psychologists as woman's No. 1 public enemies. Germaine Greer includes among women's enemies "the doctors, psychiatrists, health visitors, priests, marriage counselors, policemen, magistrates and genteel reformers."[7] Naomi Weisstein asserts, "Psychology has nothing to say about what women are really like, what they need and what they want, essentially, because psychology does not know."[8] Further, in September 1970, a group of women psychologists demanded $1 million in "reparations" from the American Psychological Association, to release women from mental hospitals and psychotherapy, where they are enslaved due to male psychology. According to Dr. Phyllis Chesler, who spoke for the group, the ethic of mental health, as defined largely by middle-aged, middle-class, white men, perceives women as "childlike, churlish, emotional, intuitive—as alien to most male psychologists."[9]

The politically focused see the ascriptions of difference leading to double standards, to abortion laws and other legal or institutional restrictions which discriminate against women and perpetuate their second-class citizenship. Like the old "separate but
equal" fiasco, assertions about the way women are, as distinct
from men, have tended to lead to assignments of place and thus
to slavery rather than liberation. Reading between the lines, one
might hazard the guess that the more psychologically inclined at
the symposium probably retained appreciation for Erikson or
Jung or Fromm even if they had gone beyond the narrower
confines of Freud's admitted mystification about women. For
them the need for sexual identity and the constructive possibility
for social roles could be contemplated in relation to psychic
health. They might be more inclined to think of a person's coming to terms with some societal expectations which aren't apt to
be discarded overnight rather than to call for the overthrow in
toto of the sexist structure we have becasue of its admittedly
undesirable features.

If we can proceed on John Stuart Mill's premise that people
are often right in what they affirm and wrong in what they deny,
it just may be that some light can be forthcoming both from a
vigorous attack on certain myths about femininity because of
their ethical questionableness and from a more sympathetic examination of some of the qualities which seem to characterize
women in general, because of nature or nurture or both, which
might have had and might promise salutary ramifications for us
all. Even if "femininity" is wholly cultural, it does not thereby
become instantly shuckable like an out-of-style coat.

In Search of the Differences

Before examining some descriptions of differences between
boys and girls and between men and women, let it be understood
from the outset that we will deal with no nursery-rhyme caricatures of "sugar and spice and everything nice" versus "frogs and

snails and puppy dog tails." Many little girls and boys may still
be clothed and counseled on that basis, but a trend toward equality of treatment is moving downward through the middle class
and into the lower economic classes, according to Urie Bronfenbrenner.[10] It should also be recognized that people who were not
masters but mastered and who were dependent for their well-
being on pleasing "the man" have developed characteristics
which have been called "naturally feminine." Gordon Allport's
classic work *The Nature of Prejudice* treats traits of victimized
people—particularly blacks and Jews—and produces a list that
sounds very "feminine." Sidney Callahan writes:

> Social analysis has shown that any group denied rights, initiative,
> education, and leadership becomes of necessity passive, depen-
> dent, intuitive, and emotional. These innate "spiritual" attributes
> have a way of disappearing with the advent of equality, as shown
> in the case of the American Negro. It is necessity, not nature, that
> has made women seek satisfaction in personal and concrete con-
> cerns rather than in aggressive abstract thought.[11]

Neither do these delineations qualify as airtight compartments. All of us stand somewhere on a continuum of femininity
and masculinity. The mix varies but every woman has her latent
masculinity and every man his latent femininity. Each sex has
recessive characteristics of the other. The two sexes begin geneti-
cally with only the single Y chromosome of the male distinguishing them, and we are commonly human more basically than we
are biologically female or male. One can even say we are all
basically female biologically, with maleness constituting an ap-
pendage (double entendre intended). Carlyle Marney, Baptist
theologian, states:

> . . . male and female are so alike as to be essentially the same.
> There is a difference but not a duality—*vive la difference!* Male-
> ness and femaleness are biological devices, not psychic equipment
> of a determinative nature. *And sex is a continuum of maleness-
> femaleness in each specimen, not a discrete entity in either.* Sex
> "traits" are so culturally determined that the social situation can

shape any sexual response from eunuch to nympho in any given infant, regardless of his biological equipment. And none is all male or purely female. Each is both from 99–1 or from 1–99, while 70–30 in favor of maleness makes a good stout burgher of the male variety. In every *fundamental* sense male and female are the same. The "duality" of male and female is not dual. We are not this discrete. . . . There is not enough real difference psychically, emotionally, or physically. To be male or female is biologically one of nature's smart packaging gimmicks, but she derived it from an original oneness which remains.[12]

Marney may have exaggerated for emphasis, but the fact is that any responsible characterizations of femininity and masculinity have to be generalizations which admit to numerous mixtures and crossovers. All of us harbor our sexual opposite both because of our genetic makeup and because of the evolution of our social selfhood in a two-sexed situation. We shall come to the Jungian understanding of contrasexuality presently.

Despite this mix in us all, we do have or need to have a sexual identity. Psychological health involves both a blending of the two in the self and an establishment of identification with the dominant sexuality one embodies, usually as seen in the parent of one's sex. Freud's genital trauma or "penis envy" theory about women becomes a distortion when applied too rigidly and universally, but it does suggest the disorder of the psychoanalytic subject who is not at home in her body because of marked maternal hostility and resultant lack of identification in the early years. Understanding that we are all somewhat androgynous keeps us from making absolute divisions of the house between masculinity and femininity, but one's basic biology still involves tendencies or proclivities which are larger than physiological in their ramifications. The "anatomy is destiny" pronouncement of Freud is "fighting words" for those who are convinced that male psychologists cannot be trusted at any age, but perhaps the meaning of destiny becomes less unmodifiable if we compare one's anatomy to being born in the Christian or post-Christian West. C. S. Lewis once wrote, "A post-Christian man is not a Pagan; you might as well think that a married woman recovers her virginity by divorce."[13] From this perspective we understand Bertrand Russell's writing "Why I Am Not a Christian," because the shape of his atheism has been destined by Christianity. The male or female does not start life with an utterly blank slate on which society chalks in manhood or womanhood *ex nihilo*. The bio-cultural interaction is much more reciprocal than that.

Anatomy is not fate, but it does destine a person to certain choices. Outside the sexual realm one could point out that a man 4 feet 11 inches in height has a choice about being a jockey but not about being a professional basketball player. A woman will always be one who decided not to have or to have children, although she might have done it the other way, and men are not destined to that childbearing choice. Freud's "anatomy is destiny" wrongly relegated all women to the nursery. Dr. Estelle Ramey suggests a more fitting understanding.

> It means that if you have ovaries, you'll never be a father. If you have testes, you'll never be a mother. . . .
>
> It does *not* mean that if you have ovaries instead of testes, you might as well forget about becoming a Senator, or a physicist, or a prime minister, or President of the United States. Or even a surgeon.[14]

In pursuit of what natural sexual differences there are, if any, one encounters descriptions of early variations which may or may not be significant. Dutch psychologist F. J. J. Buytendijk starts with bones and muscles. He calls attention to the straight lines of the male build, the right angles, the thrusting, poking, punching bodily tendencies. The female, by contrast, is rounded, curved, built to open to the other, to carry offspring, to give and receive pleasure in a different way. The difference comes to focus in the sexual organs of the convex, penetrating male, who produces attacking sperm, and the concave, receptive female with the waiting ovum.[15] The larger percentage of the male body is devoted to muscle, which could involve a tendency to greater physical exertion and pride in physical strength and skill. Edmund Overstreet, in discussing the impact of estrogen and progesterone levels, suggests that the bodily strength and endocrinologic and physiologic functioning are essentially the same for boys and girls until the age of seven, when girls begin to produce more estrogen —a difference which increases with puberty.[16]

Men have a 5 to 6 percent higher metabolic rate, and the studies of endocrinologist James B. Hamilton have led him to conclude that this higher rate causes the male to "burn out" faster and die younger. Testosterone, the male hormone, induces this slightly higher rate. Other research indicates that the female's estrogen hormones may help slow the aging of blood vessels, whereas testosterone does not—a finding which supports the growing case for women as the stronger rather than the weaker sex.[17]

The hormone balances of male and female have been shown to have other significant effects. According to Nancy R. McWilliams, a graduate student in psychology at City University of New York, studies of people with chromosomes and/or hormones of the other sex have shown them to have properties consistent with that physiology despite normal social adjustment to the reverse sex role. She is convinced that there is a hormonal impact on feeling, thinking, and acting.[18] Ashley Montagu cites the greater sexual preoccupation of women who have a disorder associated with excessive male hormones.[19] The female sexual hormone, on the other hand, has little effect on sexual desire, and when males are given it they suffer a loss of desire or potency.[20]

In 1959 Indiana University sociologist Clifford Kirkpatrick concluded that in our culture "males on the average have an earlier, a more intense, more uniform, more genital, more rhythmic, more continuous, and more promiscuous sex drive than females." One study shows the man's median age of sexual arousal as eight and the woman's as closer to sixteen. The male desire is more genitally focused, while the woman's is more diffused.[21] John Money has found that men appear to be more responsive to visual and narrative erotic stimuli and images, whereas women are more responsive to touch.[22] He found men, with their higher androgen level, more responsive and in a different way.[23] Increasing the androgen level in women heightened their capacity for arousal, but they still brought a difference in content to the response. They were not usually aroused by the pictorial image of a man, and if aroused by movies of a stripper, they had projected themselves in the position of the seductive one who desires a particular man. Kinsey found three-fourths of males aroused by portrayals of sexual action and only a third of the females.[24] Women's arousal "depends greatly on context and on an empathetic understanding of a man whereas male arousal may be simple, visual, and utterly detached from the personality of the admired person," according to McWilliams.[25] For men orgasm is bound to occur; for women it is a learned experience.[26]

There has been conjecture about the difference in sexual drive being caused by the buildup of seminal fluid and the need for discharge. But whatever the cause, there is a difference. Nancy McWilliams gets at it by observing that women do not have erections because a body passes by. Diana Trilling underlines that men are biologically capable of rape, and women are not.[27]

Differences in sexual drive, maturation, arousal, and fantasy are strongly influenced by cultural conditioning, but the documenters of differences believe that biological foundations underlie the differences and that such biological differences have substantial psychic impact. How, for instance, could it fail to shape a boy's outlook and to distinguish it from a girl's if his time of sexual arousal so far antedates hers?

Benjamin Spock may well go too far with the destiny of anatomy, but he has a point when he underlines the core problem of virility in the male which is biologically built in (on?).[28] Out of the male's fears of impotence come his dirty stories, his infidelities, his competition for jobs, his fear of losing face, his risking danger to prove himself, his aversion to asking help, and his fears of homosexuality.

Psychiatrist Erik Erikson tellingly supports the physiological roots of the feminine psychology. His pitch does not begin with "the woman's place is in the home" but with "the woman's space is in the womb." By somatic design the woman harbors an inner space which destines her to bear offspring and commits her biologically, psychologically, and ethically to caring for human infancy. Of course, a woman can reject this destiny and be at odds with her womanhood. The genital trauma theories are partial truths, but the sense of vital inner potential is more significant. Erikson is convinced that for the emotionally healthy woman who feels at home in her body, the sense of inner bodily space of productive as well as dangerous potentialities is a greater actuality to her than the lack of an external organ, which relegates her to second-class sexuality and produces "penis envy."[29]

Erikson's observations at the University of California at Berkeley of 300 ten- to twelve-year-old children, in an experiment which was not for the purpose of delineating differences of viewpoints between boys and girls, is a primary support for his view. (Critics point out that the age of the children reduces the weight of the findings.) The same experiment was tried earlier (1937) with Radcliffe students and even more recently than at Berkeley with pre-adolescent children in India. Spatial properties took on a very distinctive sexual differentiation in more than two-thirds of the scenes constructed by the children. More than two-thirds of the girls constructed interior scenes with low walls, often elaborate doors, static, peaceful conditions, and occasional animal or human male intruders. These latter were viewed humorously or with pleasurable excitement rather than with defensiveness. The boys' focus was exterior. Elaborate walls and protrusions, automated objects and animals outside in the street, and ruins and other evidences of collapse and downfall characterized the boy builders. Height, penetration, speed, collision, and explosion were common.[30] (Statistics on accidental deaths in children show, for instance, that boys go further out of the way to meet their deaths.) Erikson contends that these sexual differences are not just products of assigned social roles but are also anatomical in origin. Anatomy, then, is destiny, although it is not the sole determinant of destiny. It combines with history and personality to give us our destiny. Despite the crossovers, woman's distinctive inclination is to include, to accept, "to have and to hold," to care for, to preserve, and to restore with a quieter kind of creativity.

Harvard psychologist David McClelland sees the possibility that men and women could become psychologically indistinguishable in the future, but he also seconds Erikson's position that anatomy influences personality development if nothing reverses the normal learning. He delineates characteristic male and female styles which harmonize with those of Erikson. He cites studies which support the generalizations that the masculine life-style is rational, active, controlling; the feminine intuitive, passive, and "letting be." Men tend to be assertive, analytic, manipulative, thing-oriented; they see life as a series of episodes in which they attack their environment, tackle a problem, succeed or fail, and move on. Women are more interdependent, contextual (aware of a total situation), adjustive, responsive to influences, people-oriented; their self-image is defined by interpersonal relations rather than by leadership. McClelland alludes to the findings of Kagan and Moss concerning the effects of maternal hostility during the first three years. The girls were more apt to become tough, assertive, "masculine" women, while the boys became shy, withdrawn, and nonaggressive. Maternal protectiveness, on the other hand, produced shy, quiet girls and tough, extroverted boys.[31]

Research on infants under thirty days old has shown that infant girls spend more time looking at faces, especially human faces, and that boys prefer patterns; girls respond more to music, to color, or to a human voice, while boys show greater response to pure tones. Studies of nursery-school children by child psychologist Evelyn Goodenough Pitcher showed girls bored with brightly colored chips although boys built eagerly with them. Girls drew pictures of people, while boys drew cars, parks, trains, and only an occasional person.[32] These findings would suggest that environment is not wholly accountable for some of the college-age studies cited by McClelland which revealed that in small groups women look oftener and longer at each other's faces than men do.

Dr. Peter Wolff of Harvard has found that from birth to adulthood girls are more responsive to color than boys, able to make quicker adaptation to responses, able to shift attention quicker, able to perceive detail better, quicker to obtain oral and language skills, and able to deal with stress and adversity with more resilience. Boys are better at reconstructing concrete situations, doing abstract tasks, and separating relevant from irrelevant data.[33] McClelland cites the cross-culturally administered test developed by Whiting and others which showed that women preferred the figures in the left-hand column below in seventeen of the eighteen cultures tested when McClelland wrote in 1964.[34]

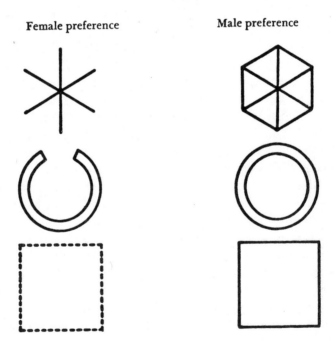

Female preference   Male preference

McClelland also cites the difference between male and female interpretations of a scene showing a male and a female acrobat in the midst of their act.[35] The men's analyses stressed reaching a climax or pinnacle of achievement with nowhere to go but down, while the women's emphasized the interdependence and relatedness of the two people. In addition he points out that sex hormones differ and affect assertiveness in other animals, that differences in mobility and sensitivity show up in newborns before culture could have taken effect, that some differences seem unrelated to role expectation, and that there must be a reason why nearly all cultures train boys assertively and girls interdependently.

Anthropologist Ashley Montagu finds in women a higher threshold to frustration and thus less tendency to aggression, greater emotional strength involving greater resilience and fewer ulcers, heart attacks (men have a 50 percent greater rate), nervous breakdowns, and suicides (three male suicides for one female as of 1970), quicker response to stimuli, greater sensitivity to environment, and better color discrimination. Later findings than his cite 15 percent more men in mental institutions and six times more drug addictions, but it is also coming to light that American women are now suffering more nervous breakdowns and related psychic disorders than men as opposed to women in poorer lands.[36] Germaine Greer cites British evidence that more women attempt suicide and more women are in mental hospitals than men, and quotes a claim that over a million British women are addicted to tranquilizers.[37]

According to Ashley Montagu, girls demonstrate less aggressiveness and quarrelsomeness in all school ages. Studies of three- to five-year-olds are cited to indicate more interest by girls in personal relationships rather than things, more responsibility and motherly behavior, and greater social competence and interest. He is convinced that women are more self-sacrificing and altruistic and less competitive. He even suggests that woman is the more advanced in evolution of the two sexes because she maintains the evolutionary promise of the fetal or infant skull more than the male.[38]

Montagu's contentions about personal relationships would receive strong backing from Daniel Casriel, psychiatrist at Daytop Village drug rehabilitation center in New York and advocate of the "liberating scream." (To aid his patients in making immediate contact with their feelings, he gets them to scream and shriek out their anguish, fear, and rage.) Casriel divides people into two groups—those who accept a human relationship no matter what the cost (80 percent of the women in our society) and those who reject a human relationship no matter what the cost (80 percent of the men in our society).[39]

These differences are discussed by some writers in terms of ways of knowing. Yale's Robert J. Lifton, in his article "Woman as Knower," suggests that "women do know something *as women*, not entirely different from what men know but in a different way." He sees in women an interest in "informal knowledge," rooted in their "close identification with organic life and its perpetuation." Women gain "insight" or "wisdom" through experiential patterns of cognition and feeling.[40] Although women have no monopoly on what Michael Polanyi calls personal knowledge, men do have a proclivity for moving on an organized abstract plane as distinguished from an organic feel for things.

Similarly, historian Lynn White, Jr., asserts that women tend toward the verbal (they read quicker), the qualitative, and the specific, whereas men have numerical, quantitative, abstract leanings. Men have a penchant for schematization and collections; women are more fascinated with the individual specimen than with completing the set of stamps, coins, etc. Characteristically, men look at "big questions," larger patterns, abstractions; women get down to cases and focus on the commonplace.[41]

On the question of verbal skills, the 1971 results of tests in writing and science, administered to youngsters of nine, thirteen, and seventeen years and to young adults over a several-year period, show boys developing a growing edge over women in science and girls developing a growing edge in writing. In both cases the edge was slight at nine and thirteen, and 3 percent at seventeen years, a finding which could support an environmental explanation for the discrepancies (depending on the impact one assigns to the onset of puberty). It is also true that males suffer from learning and behavior disorders three to ten times as often as females of the same age, that males outnumber female juvenile delinquents five to one, and that a very high percentage of juvenile delinquents have learning disorders, particularly reading disabilities such as dyslexia.

Eleanor Maccoby musters a convincing environmental case for the sex differences in verbal and math skills and spatial perception at the high school age. Girls, it turns out, who did better on the math tests and on a spatial test (adjusting a rod to a vertical position while sitting in a tilted chair or tilted room) had been left alone more and encouraged to take initiative and be independent by their mothers. Famous women mathematicians, she finds, had unusually close relationships with their fathers. High IQ girls had tomboy tendencies and low acceptance of authority. On the other hand, more verbally inclined boys as well as girls had been helped more by parents, protected more, socialized more.[42] It's hard to fault the Maccoby case, but are there tendencies which incline girls toward being more socialized? Bardwick and Douvan point to the boy's need, in our culture, to earn his masculinity early, whereas a girl's femininity does not have to be earned until puberty. Early male experience of adult sanctions against pleasurable and aggressive inclinations forces a boy to develop a sense of self and criteria of worth which are independent of others' responses.[43] Are we dealing, then, with nature or nurture or both?

Karl Stern, in *The Flight from Woman*, delineates discursive reason and intuition as scientific and poetic knowledge.[44] Scientific knowledge, which disassembles, externalizes, analyzes, symbolizes, reifies, abstracts, and projects ideas outside or above, is more identifiable with man, the penetrator and attacker and manipulator. Poetic knowledge, which intuits, feels with, participates in, internalizes, enters into, and incorporates what it knows, is more the feminine way. To borrow from Gabriel Marcel, one is more problem and solution oriented; the other is more oriented to mystery and unification.

Although feminist literature scoffs at the association of the mysterious, the affective, and the unconscious with womanhood, Stern suggests why such associations have arisen. The preconceptual, pre-rational, pre-verbal world out of which man's mode of knowing arises is inextricably tied to one's participation in the body and world of the mother. The drama of disconnection occurs before conscious reasoning, but women remain attached to the tides of nature, which cannot be hurried, to a "non-reflective bios," in unavoidable ways. Stern gives the example of the woman who became deeply depressed at the time her aborted baby would have been born, even though she did not consciously realize the coincidence of the dates. Women remain biologically and psychologically tied to nature and involved in its rhythm in ways that men do not.[45]

Alan Watts speaks of two modes of "sensitivity"—those of the "spotlight" (of conscious attention) and of the "floodlight" (of taking in without "noticing"). The latter is more preconscious, subconscious, unconscious, and superconscious. Its neglect in academia, where memory, computation, reading, and writing are elevated over social and kinesthetic intelligence, is a neglect of the feminine—"the woman in man," as Watts puts it. Four sorts of examples of the defect are mentioned: (1) the valuing of symbols (grades, money, etc.) over what they represent; (2) the noticing of things rather than contexts, backgrounds; (3) an alienation of the individual from his world, in which the personality is thought of as stopping with one's skin, and one's interconnections and solidarity with a larger social and natural environmental body are denied; (4) male mistrust of all that is feminine, and elevation of masculine symbols. (Phallic rockets attract the man who's afraid he's not a man.)[46]

Germaine Greer says that if there is a difference between

men's and women's ways of knowing, that difference may be a
lack of corruption by the characteristically male way. Whereas
Otto Weininger had criticized women for identifying thinking
and feeling, Greer suggests that this may be a freedom that
women should promote. She asks, "Can it be that women have
survived the process which debilitated the rest of male-dominated
western culture?"—the seventeenth-century dissociation of feeling and thought. We can be grateful that women often refuse to
argue logically and fail to buy the masculine notion that men are
rational animals. Clarification falsifies if it loses a sense of the
whole. Women retain a greater awareness of complexity, a more
erotic sense of reality, a greater sense of unification with the rest
of the world in contrast to the way of division, separation, par-
ticularity, and what Whitehead called "the insanity of pure intelligence." Greer sees Lao-Tse, Whitehead, Merleau-Ponty, Norman O. Brown, and Herbert Marcuse as some allies in the
elevation of a different way of comprehending. Women can then
count themselves fortunate if they manage to avoid conforming
to the going model of knowing and maintain something of the
child's ignorance. As Greer observes, "As long as education remains largely induction, ignorance will retain these advantages
over learning."[47]

The lockstep of logic has implications in morality too. Since
the Nazis are an example of those who separated feeling and
judgment, women's lack of deduction from principles should not
be automatically dubbed a moral defect. Freud said of women,
"Their superego is never so inexorable, so impersonal, so independent of its emotional origins as we require it to be in men." If
women are indeed "more often influenced in their judgments by
feelings of affection or hostility,"[48] is their sense of justice automatically deficient? Are guilt and neuroses, repressive self-nega-
tion, and aggressive environmental negation so much to be preferred to a more contextual awareness of complexity which relies
on responding to a total situation as one perceives it?

A Third Approach and a Possible Answer

Alan Watts and others have looked to Eastern religious sources such as the Tantra in India or Taoism in China for support in talking about the woman in man. Another way of moving beyond the impasse of the biology-versus-culture debate which more than one woman is finding fruitful is the symbolic approach of Jungian psychology. I am heavily indebted to Ann Belford Ulanov's *The Feminine: in Jungian Psychology and in Christian Theology* for a far better grasp of this approach than I got from reading some of Jung's own writing. Penelope Washbourne is another theologian who is pursuing this line of exploration. Combining personal psychological bisexuality with a stress on sexual polarity (not polarization) between the sexes, the Jungian conception of sexuality and selfhood puts the "feminine" question in a different perspective. As Ulanov observes, the biological and cultural approaches both understand the feminine as belonging to females only. Jung's symbolic approach makes the feminine "a psychic element quite apart from its biological or cultural existence, however much it may influence or be influenced by that existence." For him, "To be without sexual distinctions would be to be without psychical structure." Ulanov also asserts that there is a contrast in the content of the descriptions of the feminine among the three approaches.[49]

The basic reality with which psychology, Jungian or otherwise, deals is the psyche, which "consists of energy, consciousness, the personal unconscious, and the collective unconscious or the objective psyche."[50] This psyche for Jung is structured in polarities. The tensions of these polarities generate a dynamism called libido which is the very energy of life. Among the opposing tendencies of the psyche are conscious-unconscious, inner-outer, reason-instinct, finite-infinite, intellect-imagination, empirical-mysterious, and active-passive, but the masculine-feminine polarity encompasses all the others in its symbolism. In most psychoanalytic literature the feminine is seen as tangent to the masculine and confined to its literal sexuality. Jung, in contrast, "explores the feminine as a distinct category of being and a mode of perception *inherent in all men, all women, and all culture*."[51] The polarity is experienced both in relation to members of the opposite sex and in one's experience of oneself. The contrasexual element in the male psyche is called the "anima" and in the female the "animus."

For Jung, the "self" is the total personality which synthesizes the ego (the center of consciousness) with the psyche, which acts on us as an objective "other"—even a personal other. We remain ignorant of the psyche's nature, since we know it indirectly, and it cannot properly be reduced to one's consciousness of it. This objective reality is made perceptible through symbols, which convey to the person its quality, intention, and effect on the whole personality. Fantasies and dreams then point to what the unconscious is saying by pointing to archetypes which are not experienced per se. Dreams, patterns of behavior, and symptoms also provide Jung with means of inferring the structure of this unconscious facet of the self. The ego becomes aware of the contents of the unconscious through complexes—clusters of ideas and images around an archetypal image (e.g., a "mother complex").[52] As Ulanov explains, "At the core of every complex is a transpersonal, universally human pattern of experience."[53] In the case of the mother archetype, its negative aspects are felt as devouring and castrating; its positive aspects as enfolding and nurturing. This primordial image lies dormant in the psyche until some challenge triggers a confrontation. A complex may be pathological, or it may provide a fruitful and needed source of energy.

The ego is the central complex of the psyche and relates the psyche both to outer reality and to inner subjective reality. Its cluster of functions (willing, choosing), images (of person and the world), and feelings (toward oneself and others) gather around the archetypal core of the self. Anima, animus, and shadow are also psychic complexes or clusters. The "shadow" symbolizes the psychic mediation between the ego and the personal unconscious (composed of once-conscious content). It refers to the projection of the darker or negative aspects of one's personality as another force which is recognized and included by the healthy personality. Personified as the devil on the collective level and as a disliked person of our sex on the individual level, our shadow is usually met first as a projection on others of what we cannot accept in ourselves.[54]

The symbolic concepts Jung used to describe the psychic mediation between the collective unconscious (the deeper layer which is usually inaccessible to consciousness) and the personal unconscious—between the universal archetypes expressed in myths and primordial images and one's own repressed memories and complexes—are "anima" for men and "animus" for women. The otherness of the deeper objective psyche comes to the surface in consciousness in images of the opposite sex—probably because the opposite sex provides the most impressive early experience of otherness.

The anima is represented in myths having to do with the eternal feminine in all its forms—Mother Earth, love, or wisdom; and it has a wide range of images—harlot, witch, martyr, sister, peasant, gypsy, beloved, muse, saint, goddess, spiritual guide. Animus images include laborer, judge, teacher, monk, Prince Charming, prophet, magician, rapist. The witches, fairy godmothers, Prince Charmings, Snow Whites, forests, dogs, and good and bad kings in fairy stories are thus seen as more than the products of the imagination. They are projections of images from the unconscious. Ulanov's book, for instance, includes a fascinating discussion of *The Wizard of Oz* story as a tracing of Dorothy's psychic development. On the personal side these symbols reflect the influences of actual women in a man's life and vice versa. On the objective or archetypal side, they personify the universal or transpersonal experiences of the contrasexual pole. Anima personifies such "feminine" qualities as "tenderness, sensitivity, deviousness, seduction, indefiniteness, feeling, receptivity, elusiveness, jealousy, and creative containing and yielding." The animus symbolizes such elements as active initiative, aggressive assertiveness, the search for meaning, creativity, and a capacity for discrimination, separation, and judgment.[55]

To establish contact with his anima a man must treat her personally as an actual inner woman. But to develop a relationship with his anima he must get beyond the women in his life to the transpersonal energy and meaning of the feminine archetypes which lie deep within. When he is receptive toward this complex it ceases to be personified and becomes a means of relating the conscious to the unconscious in himself, of opening him to previously inaccessible capacities in himself. The same is true of the woman and her animus. Problems result when consciousness (I, ego) is identified with, not differentiated from, the "other" subsidiary contrasexual personality. Instead of enrichment for the self through a dynamic interaction of masculine and feminine, what occurs is a rejection of one's biological sexuality for an opposite sexual identity. In men, touchiness, sentimentality, and effeminacy to the point of homosexuality can occur. A man may become seduced by his anima and experience an inflated self-image. A woman's partial identity with her animus may be expressed in a ruthless egotism masked by compliance and helplessness or a primitive urge for prestige which crushes anything that interferes with good appearances.[56]

Ulanov points out that group movements which urge women to form sexual collectives as a means to independence from men do not recognize the tyranny that animus judgments are exerting over them.

> They are still subjectively dependent on the masculine elements of their own personalities because they have not sufficiently developed or related to the animus function. Instead of becoming independent of the masculine, they grow more and more unconscious of the animus and project its tyranny onto all men.[57]

They also, we should add, remain largely peripheral and irrelevant to the larger scheme of things they want to change.

Either sex may also project the other (animus or anima) as an opposite sex to which no one can ever measure up. Contact is diminished between the conscious and the unconscious by such defenses as repression of the contrasexual pole or breaking into a split personality.[58]

Archetypal images are not themselves inherited. What all people are equipped with are instinctual potentialities or systems of readiness for action, images, and emotions. This potentiality is given specific content which is not inherited and which differs according to cultural context.

> The form [of the archetype] manifests itself dynamically as a pattern of behavior and emotional reaction. It manifests itself representationally as images, personifications, and motifs that are recorded in myths on the collective level and in dreams and visions on the individual level.[59]

Dealing with such occurrences as dreams and visions, the Jungian method attempts to "bring about a conscious ego encounter with relation to archetypal material," which has constructive as well as destructive possibilities. The Great Mother is an archetype which manifests the feminine and has both nourishing and devouring capacities. The Spiritual Father archetype has positive aspects such as law, order, discipline, rationality, understanding, and inspiration, but its negative aspects may lead to alienation from reality and ego inflation.

As Ulanov summarizes:

> In Jung's view, psychological development is the progressive differentiation of the ego, or consciousness, from unconsciousness and the building of a cooperative relationship between the ego and the unconscious and especially between the ego and the archetypal images that underlie the evolution of the human psyche.[60]

Further, the significance of contrasexuality in all this is that one moves toward psychological wholeness or integrity by coming to terms consciously with the opposite sex we all contain within ourselves.

Jung and such followers as Erich Neumann, Michael Fordham, and Edward Edinger have delineated certain phases of psychological development. In the early phase, which corresponds to
the prenatal period and early infancy, the ego exists in undifferentiated, unconscious identity with the world of archetypes within
and the external world without. LSD trips provide later examples
of these feelings. The second stage, corresponding to early child-
hood, is called matriarchal by Neumann. The newly emerged ego
has only indistinct consciousness, and it is still passively dependent on the unconscious (personified by the Great Mother). A
male homosexual's common subservience to the mother (human
and archetypal) is an example of remaining in this stage. In place
of pre-sexual contented wholeness, the budding ego is conscious
of otherness. The sexual polarity comes to stand for differentiation, for the experience of the other sex, the unconscious, and
God.[61]

It is worth noting that these two pre-ego phases of psychological development are the same for both sexes but are experienced very differently by each. The boy experiences opposing
sexual elements sooner because his relation to his mother is that
of like to unlike. Ulanov says:

> His self-discovery takes place in opposition to the primary relation-
> ship with the mother, and this effects a greater isolation through
> its new emphasis upon objectivity and ego consciousness.[62]

Only after he establishes his freedom from the mother can he
resume his relation to the unconscious. Girls' early identity with
the mother involves a drawing of like to like. The danger is
fixation, not castration, since a girl's ego development takes place
in relation, not opposition, to her unconscious. Her instinctive
way of relating, then, is through identification—not discrimination.

Neumann's third stage is patriarchal (prepuberty and early
puberty years). The Great Father is now sovereign deity. The
feminine is rejected. Consciousness, rationality, willpower, self-

discipline, and individual responsibility are highly valued. Separation of the ego has replaced participation in the original totality. Inner-outer, subject-object, and right-wrong are clear distinctions. Ulanov summarizes:

> . . . the principle of spirit is seen as opposed to earth; order and definition are seen as superior to creative fertility, commandments and obedience are valued over the virtues of acceptance and forgiveness, and becoming is seen as better than "just being."[63]

The fourth phase or stage is called integrative. Now the nonrational, emotive feminine (woman, unconscious anima) is reunited with the ego.[64] Opposites are reconciled—masculine and feminine, law and love, conscious and unconscious, spirit and nature. For the woman, the masculine assumes a personal form. Archetypically a hero (animus or outer man) frees the daughter from bondage to the father and establishes an equal relation with her.[65] According to Ulanov, outwardly the integrative stage of Neumann usually issues in marriage of a Western patriarchal sort. (Jung uses the label "medieval.") What unfortunately happens for this brand of marriage is that each sex gives up his or her own natural psychological contrasexuality. Man's anima is projected on the woman and vice versa. Roles are divided—each sex is dependent on the other. Polarization, due to a fear of otherness, replaces the recognition of a polarity, an otherness in one's self. Marriage is a reasonable agreement instead of an intimate sharing. The feminine role is narrowly defined, and the animus tyrannizes, either as a fantasy ideal or as a projection on some social cause or movement to which the woman dedicates herself fanatically. Deep disillusionment with the male may also result from fixation at this stage; there may be a regression to the matriarchal phase. Lack of fulfillment with the husband makes a devouring mother vis-à-vis her children.

Fixation at the first stage is self-conservation. At the second it is self-surrender. At the third stage it is self-loss. All these have positive and negative possibilities, even in the latter case. There a partnership with a male may loose her from unconscious containment within the masculine, but she may have her own development arrested by confining herself to a patriarchal caricature of the feminine.[66]

The crown of psychological development is the process of individuation, in which the ego is replaced by the self as the center of personality. The ego is not abolished or consigned to its pre-emergent containment in the unconscious, but it discovers its limits. The person becomes a separate whole; but individuation is not individualism. The ego sees itself in the larger context of the intentions of the whole psyche. What it serves is more important than the values which merely serve it. The opposing poles are reconciled in a third form. There is a "religious" experience of relating to a larger center of the self.

The phase of feminine development which corresponds to individuation is "marked by stages of confrontation and individuation, by self-discovery, and by self-giving."[67] The woman ceases to project her animus on the man; it becomes an inner function of her own psyche; she develops an ego identity which actively relates to the feminine self. If a marriage is to reach this phase, the purely masculine man and the purely feminine woman give way to two fully participating partners. Joe Namath and Raquel Welch leave the scene to ordinary people like us whose physiques and personalities bear only occasional resemblances to the "images" of the sex symbols, no matter how much we invest in padded bras, brutishly enticing skin bracers, and other stereotyped role cultivations.

> True confrontation occurs only after each partner has recovered his own contrasexual unconscious nature. Each can then relate out of a whole nature to the wholeness of the other.[68]

The experience of confrontation still differs for the sexes. Man's assimilation of the feminine is private, initiated by his anima or a woman, not by culture. A woman, though, has had to develop masculinity in a patriarchal culture. In her case, the animus does not urge confrontation, but rather the self—which is feminine. Interestingly then, the feminine initiates this confrontation and individuation in both sexes. The feminine is the completing element for both sexes![69]

Jungian Toni Wolff suggests four structural forms of the feminine: the Mother, the Hetaira (companion), the Amazon, and the Medium. Each of these types has a dominant archetype which can be positive or negative, a certain pattern of identity, and a typical way of relating to man and to the animus. The Mother has the Great Mother (helping or devouring) as dominant archetype, an identity which is either nourishing or masochistic, a mothering relation to man, and a relation to the animus as eternal son. The animus may remain an inner revolutionary or be projected as unrealized creativity onto a son. This type has fixated at a stage which corresponds with the first two phases of psychological development.

The Hetaira has the Great Father archetype and may either relate to it in the psyche or submerge herself in identification with the father's anima.[70] She may be awakened as an individual or play the role of the temptress who lures others away from adapting to reality. She relates to men as a little girl, a daughter, and makes the animus a hero who frees or ravages her. She passively identifies with her animus. It may replace the ego function and tyrannize her. She feels alive only with or through a man. Unconsciously she tyrannizes over the man by preferring his feelings and actions to hers. This form is similar to a fixation at the patriarchal stage.

The teachings of an anti-women's-liberation corporation called Fascinating Womanhood, which is based in Santa Barbara, California, offer a caricature of this stage. The F.W. classes teach "childlikeness" and "sauciness" for the improvement of the marriage. One follower says,

> When I can't handle things in my marriage . . . I say to Greg, "Oh, I'm just a little girl," and it works! And you know what

helps? To look at your own little girl—the way she "stamps her foot and shakes her curls," you just want to love her![71]

The latest book of Helen B. Andelin, whose husband, Aubrey P. Andelin, is president of the "Foundation," is *The Fascinating Girl.*

The Amazon has the Virgin for a dominant archetype, which may mean she is self-contained or that she is downright cold and cut off from feeling. Her identity can be either her own ego's development or an identification with the shadow or animus of the mother. She relates to men as a comrade, colleague, or competitor, and her animus is personified as a father who is either a spiritual guide or a tyrant.

The Medium's Wise Woman archetype can either further culture or further evil (witch). Her identity may display a firm ego with powers of discrimination or a lost ego in the collective unconscious. She relates to man as Mediatrix and her animus is experienced as Wise Man or tempting Magician. Our present culture offers the widest range to the Amazon and Mother. In antiquity, the Middle Ages, and the Renaissance, the Companion and Medium had strong cultural support.[72]

This summary of Ulanov's summary of Jung's thought has no doubt left the already knowledgeable offended and the not yet knowledgeable confused. However, it all seemed necessary to set in context the centrality of sexual polarity in Jung's thought. Ulanov is convinced that the restoration to men of what is feminine and to women of what is masculine would at the same time make men more, not less, masculine and women more feminine. For both it would mean the recovery of a fullness of interiority, a full spiritual life, and a true sense of the human person, which have been lost with the neglect of the feminine. Otherwise, unclaimed sexual identity can affect the unconscious contrasexual element. A mannish woman may have an effeminate animus and thus be attracted to homosexual men. An effeminate man often has a warrior anima, which he projects on all women.[73]

Ulanov urges that positing a stable structure of the psyche does not mean that the feminine pole is reducible to certain fixed characteristics (passivity, etc.) which define what a woman should be. She explains:

> In Jung's approach, the feminine is understood symbolically as an archetype which cannot be directly known in itself and therefore cannot impose a set of characteristics on individual persons.[74]

Jung describes the feminine principle as eros (psychic relatedness) in contrast to logos (objective interest). This principle is an unconscious urge to relate, to join, to reach out to, to get in touch with, to get involved with concrete feelings, things, and people, rather than to abstract or theorize. This drive operates on and in all persons, especially female persons. This principle has an elementary or static aspect which is represented as an enclosing, receptive, dark, womblike world of formation. Positively symbolized as the good mother, it effects feelings of security and acceptance. Negatively symbolized as the terrible mother it is ensnaring, devouring, paralyzing, down-dragging. There is also an active, transformative side of the feminine principle which urges change, produces ecstasy, moves out of the self to merger. Positively it is symbolized in birth-rebirth images and produces feelings of excitement, zest, vitality, inspiration, playfulness, risk. Negatively, one can experience opaqueness instead of inspiration, loss of focus instead of comprehensive vision, madness instead of growth, drunkenness, and loss of identity in the unconscious. Witches and devilish temptresses are associated symbols.[75]

Ulanov refers again to Erich Neumann, who calls feminine consciousness "matriarchal" and the feminine style of ego functioning the "heart-ego," in contrast to the masculine patriarchal "head-ego." The head-ego separates flesh and spirit. The heart-ego comprehends by accepting, assimilating, allowing something to ripen. It attends, contemplates, waits. Time is qualitative for it; it is periodic, rhythmic, favorable or unfavorable, waxing and waning.[76] The dangers are that it may "moon" aimlessly or become melancholy, dreaming, fearing, or masochistic.

> For the feminine ego, impulses of the spirit make themselves known through material things, whether it is the material of unconscious processes, of the transformations of the body such as menstruation, conception, the climacteric, or of individual moments of concrete experience of other kinds. The personal interiority of a woman is the vessel in which she touches the spirit and is touched by it, just as her body is the vessel of her physical transformation and all its openings places of exchange between inner and outer experience.[77]

We shall come presently to some theological implications of the feminine principle. Hopefully, enough has been said to reveal some of the similarities between the Jungian rendition of the feminine and some of the delineations of a feminine way of being in the world and relating to it which we have already mentioned. Some of the strengths of the Jungian approach are its assertions of the need of both sexes for a contrasexual confrontation which is enabled in both sexes by the feminine, and its moving beyond the whole hassle over whether there is an Eternal Feminine which women are bound to embody without denying a dynamic sexual polarity in life.

In using Jung's animus and anima suggestions, we do not have to subscribe to the notion that the masculine and feminine archetypes are mere transmissions from the past collective unconscious of the race. We can put the emphasis on the two-sexed character of the ordinary child's social world which is ingrained before he or she knows it. The self is social. It depends for its self-consciousness and for communication with others on that otherness in the self which is created through the penetration of the self by others. The Jungian approach indicates that the self's inner dialogue is constituted not just by social otherness but by sexual otherness.

In light of the Jungian perspective, Thomas Harris' book *I'm OK—You're OK* may have to have a sexual sequel. He has popularized the analysis of human selfhood which recognizes the presence of a Parent (internalized societal demands), a Child (spontaneous emotions), and an Adult in the person. He urges both the avoidance of confusing one with the other and the concession of sovereignty to Parent or Child by the Adult. Exchanges of communication can be analyzed with Harris' labels to clarify who is speaking to whom. We may fail to communicate because we fail to recognize, for instance, that my Parent is speaking to your Child or my Child to your Adult. Our failures to affirm each other's "OK-ness" are tied to our failure to relate on appropriate levels and to discern the ways we are missing each other.

What we may need to add are tools of analysis to clarify Daughter-Father, Mother-Son, Companion-Companion, Competitor-Competitor, Snow White–Prince Charming dimensions in transactions with persons of the opposite sex. Adult-Adult relations involve not allowing take-over by an archetypal role, but neither can these dimensions of heterosexual interaction be removed even if we try. To recognize them is not for the purpose of elimination but of affirmation and transcendence. It's not sick for a wife to mother her husband or for there to be an element of pursuit and conquest in a relationship, but it is disasterous if a relationship is taken over by archetypal images of manhood and womanhood.

Downing and Defending the Differences

Having mustered this much support for male-female differences, I have no desire to play into the hands of efforts to keep women in a condition of second-class citizenship or to engage in the kind of pedestal pushing or mystique selling which makes women too "other" to be human or too typical to be personal. Nor do I wish to join up with those Betty Friedan has dubbed "female chauvinists" because their bitterness has erupted in man-hating assertions of women's superiority and advocacies of separatism.[78] What I have described is a distinction, not a subordination, and what we must ask is whether sameness is essential to the equality women so justly seek.

Critics of "the eternal feminine" rightly fear that exaggerated emphases on the duality of the sexes, especially the utter otherness of women, have undermined the sharing of a personal relationship. Sexual union becomes a conjunction of two metaphysical principles instead of two people. Such differences in the sexual experience and response of each are assigned that one fulfills roles instead of being spontaneous and active in the expression of love. The likeness which is necessary to genuine knowledge of and communion with another is obscured by auras of mystery and ascriptions of otherness. Sidney Callahan, in both *The Illusion of Eve* and *Exiled to Eden,* has made telling criticisms of the accentuation of difference. She probably cringed if she read Norman Mailer's assertion that women are "a step, or a stage, or a move, or a leap nearer the creation of existence."[79]

"Opposite sex" thinking makes the sexual act a bodily conquest of or submission to the wholly other. Or it may mystically glorify the sexual act as the supreme "I-Thou" union with Reality. Either way, Callahan urges that the unique individuals—Fred and Sallie or Jane and Richard—are depersonalized; the partner becomes an object, a means either of sexual release or of mystical elevation. Herbert Richardson observes that the aggressiveness of sex increases in proportion to the radical difference one ascribes to the opposite sex. Seduction and conquest go then with radical differentiation.[80]

Betty and Theodore Roszak argue that many of the feigned differences between masculinity and femininity amount to deceitful and unhealthy role playing in which one is supposed to admire or desire the member of the opposite sex for what one fears or despises in herself or himself. Each desires the other for something which cannot be admitted in the self, and we are back to the failure to love the other as a person instead of as a representative of masculinity or femininity, which is in this case depicted as a kind of covert self-love. The acting of the man aggravates the acting of the woman and vice versa. As the Roszaks express it,

> He is playing the kind of man that she thinks the kind of
> woman she is playing ought to admire. She is playing the kind of
> woman that he thinks the kind of man he is playing ought to
> desire.[81]

Callahan calls for an androgynous ideal in which each sex
is free to develop and express those admirable qualties which are
often asserted to belong to the other sex naturally. Women can
be assertive and men sensitive, for instance, without anxiety or
guilt because of hang-ups about femininity and masculinity. She
urges:

> If there is such a thing as innate sexual characteristics of personal-
> ity (which seems doubtful), then Christians should strive to go
> beyond them by incorporating and cultivating the opposite quali-
> ties too.[82]

Herbert Richardson's term for this androgynous ideal is
"psychological bisexuality." This understanding of "how the
other half lives" which makes men more feminine and women
more masculine only became possible in modern times when love
became "the experience of psychological intimacy." Conversation is the key. It did not take place between men and women
in pre-modern societies, and without it one cannot tell the other
how he or she feels. The development of courtly love was a big
factor in the evolution of love toward psychological intimacy
because conversation was central to that tradition. From A.D.
1300 to 1700 self-consciousness emerged in the West. This self-
awareness brought with it a capability of changing the self and its
world and of knowing other selves "from inside out." A new union
of love and sex occurred in relationships between men and
women. The possibilities of genuine intimacy and thus for psychological bisexuality have grown with the permeation of the
modern consciousness. Richardson sees in this evolution a growing chance for personal communion rather than orgasm to be the
aim of sex and for love to rule the sex drive.[83]

On the other side there are the convictions of the Jungians

that the sexual polarity within the person and between persons is a source of dynamic creativity. Polarization of the sexes is sick, but the polarity of masculine and feminine is healthy. Rollo May is among those who take issue with the *egalitarianism* of the sexes and the *interchangeability* of sexual roles. He writes:

> Egalitarianism is clung to at the price of denying not only biological differences—which are basic, to say the least—between men and women, but emotional differences from which come much of the delight of the sexual act. The self-contradiction here is that the compulsive need to prove you are identical with your partner means that you repress your own unique sensibilities—and this is exactly what undermines your own sense of identity. This contradiction contributes to the tendency in our society for us to become machines even in bed.[84]

Nancy McWilliams is one of many who have expressed the fear that in the midst of their fierce assertions about undifferentiated equality between the sexes, many women have been taken in by masculine models of selfhood. In many reactions against the intellectual versus emotional polarization, the assumption seems to be that intellectual output should get the highest acclaim and that interpersonal sensitivity is a refuge of the weak. In reactions against Freudian suggestions that women generally have weaker superegos than men, the assumption seems to be that women are therefore morally inferior. It just may be that they are less hung up on preserving images, meeting standards, and obeying authority (inner or outer), and more oriented toward preserving relationships, meeting needs, and being true to others. McWilliams is convinced that much of women's oppression is due to their internalization of masculine values, through the educational system, for instance. "Women themselves undervalue the best qualities of womanhood," she says.[85]

From both directions comes a concern lest the personhood and uniqueness of the self be undermined. One attacks the practice of both men and women in viewing each woman, even the self, as the Eternal Feminine. The other sees that some determined attempts at rejection of the Eternal Feminine have merely resulted in the substitution of a caricatured male model for women as the way to be human. Simone de Beauvoir's classic study *The Second Sex* has been justly criticized for making masculinity the model of humanity, but even this disparager of her own femaleness could write:

> . . . there will always be certain differences between man and woman; her eroticism, and therefore her sexual world, have a special form of their own and therefore cannot fail to engender a sensuality, a sensitivity, of a special nature. This means that her relations to her own body, to that of the male, to the child, will never be identical with those the male bears to his own body, to that of the female, and to the child; those who make much of "equality in difference" could not with good grace refuse to grant me the possible existence of the differences in equality.[86]

On the other hand, when fears are voiced lest a woman sell her feminine birthright for a mess of masculine pottage out of a desire to continue things as they are, it is no wonder that women feel that they are being asked not to get into the important action under a pretense of concern for them and for their cherished virtues.

Evolving Sexuality and the Androgynous Ideal

Increasingly it appears that neither the male sex nor the female sex nor the society we constitute can remain the same. What is happening and what is needed is an evolution toward something neither men nor women have a corner on alone. Many now assert that in the world of the future men are going to need to change more in a feminine direction than women are in a masculine direction. In this light and in view of the Jungian insights on the polarity in each of us, a more androgynous ideal should not be seen as the abolition of all differences between the sexes. It calls, rather, for the outgrowing of anxiously exaggerated models of male *machismo* with their requisite counterpart models of a femininity which lacks any wholeness of its own and can only live through the male. The concern, then, is that whole people be able to enter relationships with other whole people rather than as defective halves who don't start living until they are sweethearts, wives, and mothers. Such a relationship would be one in which men and women could more readily become like each other without being totally absorbed by each other. They could evoke and have evoked that other sexuality in themselves without anxiety.

Erik Erikson's stages in the life cycle point up the fact that a sense of identity must precede the capacity for genuine intimacy. Significantly the adolescent stage, which is critical for the achievement of a sense of ego identity and avoidance of identity diffusion, is also the stage when the youth's sexuality comes to focus in genital sexuality. In healthy, normal development the discovery or pulling together of one's identity involves the acceptance of oneself as a sexual being and the development of confidence in one's ability to relate to members of the opposite sex.

When a sexual identity is well established it is most capable of being transcended—not denied. Abraham H. Maslow found that healthy, fulfilled mates made no sharp differentiation between sex roles in sexual play. The men were sure of their maleness and the women of their femaleness, and they did not limit the active role to the men and the passive to the women. Neither did they self-consciously hold out for side-by-side egalitarianism in intercourse. Men were generally more assertive, and both enjoyed man's being in a position to effect maximum union of the bodies in the climactic phase of intercourse. This seemed to satisfy the woman's deep need to feel desired.[87]

Sidney Callahan draws an apt conclusion about adding to rather than negating a basic sexual identity:

> ... since sexuality is an important way of human development and self-knowledge, it seems highly probable that male or female identity is transfigured and completed rather than superceded or suppressed.[88]

Shall We Demythologize Sex?

All of us find our identity in the context of stories. We live stories which give meaning and significance to our lives. We act in a drama, the available roles of which constitute our choices. Definitions of myth proliferate endlessly and vary greatly. One broad attempt is Daniel Maguire's:

> [Myth] is a complex of feelings, attitudes, symbols, memories, and experienced relationships through which reality is refracted, filtered, and interpreted . . . Myth is one mental mechanism that serves to give meaning.[89]

The word "myth" properly refers to those stories or complexes of images which provide the larger metaphysical context or the fundamental beliefs about man, the world, and perhaps God for the histories of ourselves and our communities. Harvey Cox puts it aptly when he calls *myth* "the symbolic definition of man's place and purpose in the scheme of things."[90]

The Creation and Fall stories of Genesis and the eschatological visions of Revelation set a larger context not only for the history of Israel, which is itself part of the Christian's myth, but also for the current Christian's understanding of himself in relation to nature, man, and God. You don't have to be a Christian to have a myth, a fundamental sense of reality which is statable in story. Modern science has its basic mythology which informs its efforts, and there are numerous sexual myths which shape profoundly the stories we live out. The myth of romantic love, the Playboy mythology, and the *Küche, Kirche, Kinder* mythology about womanhood are a few examples. Our views of our sexuality and our relations to other sexual beings are profoundly shaped by a variety of myths.

Some discussions of myth would imply that we should get rid of them and view things "objectively" and "scientifically" and "realistically." *Myth* then is virtually equated with illusion. However, the fact is that one never can render himself mythless. We never approach the data of experience with a blank slate, and if we did they would make no sense. We reject one myth or set of myths only out of preference for influence by another myth. If the Jungian analysis of myth as the means of expression of universal feminine and masculine archetypes is valid, we get at the reality of our sexual polarity not by scuttling myths but by coming to understand them as expressions of unconscious dimensions of the psyche.

The problem is to sort out which myths illuminate experience and which distort our vision of reality. For instance, archetypal images have both creative and destructive potentialities. We can't sterilize ourselves of myth, but that doesn't mean that one myth is as good as the next. The Nazi mythology of the master race, the myths of racism, and the mythologies of American know-how and the self-made man are hardly comparable. The Nazi ideology and that of white supremacy were never anything better than excuses for the subjugation by one group of another group. The self-made man and American know-how myths have had very constructive and beneficial effects in frontier society and scientific advancement. However, the limitations and dangers of these myths have become obvious to us now. The Horatio Alger story could be a spur to realize one's potentialities, but it could end in an economic philosophy which was aptly rendered by Bishop Charles Gore's wry critique: "Each for himself and God for us all, as the elephant said when he danced among the chickens." The myth of American ingenuity put men on the moon, but it also put the foreign policy in our heads of which Vietnam is the ugly outcome. We were so sure that if we put our minds, men, and material to it we could save Vietnam from the evils of communism, teach it democracy, and enable it to develop in our image. Little did this mythology reckon with the very different mythologies of the people of Vietnam. These are examples, then, of myths which are appropriate in some contexts and not in others, which can be both socially beneficial in some instances and morally suspect in others.

In this light, what shall we say about our sexual myths? Some of them have obviously been unmitigated evils. The cruelties that have been visited on girls and women (as well as boys and men, though to a far lesser extent) of both a physical and a psychic nature because of sexual myths may have been "functional" sociologically in some way, but they must still be written off as inhuman. The performing of clitoridectomies on young girls and the burning of widows on funeral pyres and "witches" at the stake just won't come out in the wash of cultural relativism. There are, however, so-called sexist myths which are far from being all bad, even though they may be dated or in need of qualification by greater awareness of mythical pluralism. The "motherhood myth" undoubtedly has foreclosed career possibilities for many girls, but it is also true that it has given a sense of meaning to many and that it has often provided that meaning in situations where other possibilities were either nonexistent or exceedingly scarce. Faced with the population explosion and with expanding opportunities for women, we can be pleased that the "motherhood myth" is becoming an option rather than a culturally indoctrinated requirement for every woman. However, the wholesale discarding of the myth can have effects that are anything but self-evidently desirable.

How eagerly would we look forward to a society in which little girls did not see enough of their mothers for them to be viable identity models? In raising children shall we attempt to rear girls who do not cultivate the nurturing instincts or acquire the nurturing traits as they play with dolls and play house? My wife and I are concerned that our girls not think of themselves solely that way and that they not think of their mother solely as a homemaker. However, it will be a sad day if and when most of the people who could be the ablest parents and most creative homemakers have drawn the conclusion which is implicit in many feminist writings, i.e., it takes a pea brain to find any meaning and satisfaction in the traditional roles of mother and housewife even for a part of one's life. Ti-Grace Atkinson's call for the annihilation of all sex roles and for the end of uterine pregnancy would seem to be as questionable as the assertion that women who don't have babies are doomed to remain unfulfilled. Betty Friedan gets some of her sisters told quite well: "A female chauvinism that makes a woman apologize for loving her husband or children— or that defines self-fulfillment as a contradiction of her womanly self as a wife or mother, instead of *including* it—denies the real feelings of too many women."[91]

It will be many a day before most couples have the option of splitting the in-house work and the breadwinning work on a fifty-fifty basis, and one shudders at the prospect of a generation of well-educated women who wouldn't touch children, homemaking, cooking, and maybe even marriage with a ten-foot pole. Women are entitled to options, and the "empty nest" problems and the "beauty parlor syndrome" highlight the need to have a larger identity than a traditional role often affords. Still, we do well to be careful about simply discarding all the old myths under the assumption that anything that is opposite to or different from them is inevitably better.

What shall we say about the myths of masculinity and femininity at the time of adolescent identity crisis? We can readily do without the Miss America mythology, which is the despair of girls with figures that deviate from ideal proportions and the boon of the cosmetic and foundation-garment industries. Hopefully the day will come when the average woman does not spend two hours of the day (as some adolescent girls now spend most of their waking hours) just on grooming. We can also work for a time when some men will not feel that they need to dress as women in order to be able to go to a movie and cry, and when violence will not be so commonly motivated by a desire to prove one's masculinity. The societal definitions of masculinity and femininity in terms of hair and dress, which are breaking down under the impact of the unisexual trend in the youth culture, are ridiculous caricatures.

Sexuality and Identity

The need still remains for the adolescent with his or her budding genitality to discover an identity as a sexual being, to feel at home in his or her body, to come to think of himself or herself as capable of fulfilling the roles which generally occupy one's sex. Should it then be surprising that a more exaggerated polarization of the sexes might be necessary and healthy in adolescence than would be desirable in later years? When one is sure of himself or herself as a budding man or woman, he is then secure enough to be intimate with another and to have something of the other rub off. It is the person whose masculinity or femininity is believed in by himself or herself and by others who is free to do and be things which are often called characteristic of the other sex. The husband who is staying home and caring for his baby while his wife works finds himself considered no less masculine and even envied by those less sure of their identities. George Blanda cried after the Oakland Raiders lost in the Sugar Bowl, and it seemed manly enough because his manliness is so well established. Granted that some people flee to homosexuality in reaction against exaggerated images of masculinity (in the case of men) or femininity (in the case of women) which they can't or won't fit, is it not also possible that "role playing" of a somewhat exaggerated sort is helpful as the adolescent searches for identity? Roles are, as James Nelson suggests, "indispensable to the identity of the social self," although "identity is not the sum total of one's roles." Speaking specifically to the matter under discussion, he writes, "As a matter of fact, most married women seeking greater personal fulfillment search for it *through* additional roles and not apart from them."[92] No doubt the stereotypes of the football hero and Miss America have often done more to heighten anxieties about identity than to provide defined roles to try on, but will there not need to be a sexual coloring to the identity models which adolescents try on at a time when their sexuality looms so large? The finding of this happy medium is the dilemma we face.

How can we selectively modify or discard or outgrow some myths and preserve or create others to effect the achievement of a sexual identity which is ready for true intimacy?

These myths, models, and roles will need to be more plural and more flexible than they have usually been in the past. People need room for choice and growth and change. Just as one of the dehumanizing aspects of the so-called Protestant work ethic has been that occupations have become preoccupations, and people have literally lost themselves in their work, so women have felt that they have lost themselves by being totally defined by their husband and children. The best answers, though, aren't found for frustrated women when they reject a one-dimensional, home-defined existence for a one-dimensional, work-defined existence. In a day when a series of occupations rather than a life-long job is becoming increasingly common, and the amount of leisure time for many is expanding, the ability many women have developed to combine familial relationships and jobs (without the near total sacrifice of one to the other) and to develop an identity based on a combination of relationships can be the wave of the future. Deferring a career outside the home for parenthood or deferring parenthood for an outside career is a vastly different choice if the choice is not seen as permanent or merely a necessary evil to be endured. Diana Trilling has this to say on the subject of important activity:

> . . . living by one's deference to the needs of those one loves is one of the pleasanter modes of existence—as well as, I might add, one of the most taxing. It is a grave fault of modern culture that it trains us in the belief that whatever defers to others is an *in*action and therefore of only secondary social value.[93]

Footnote for Fathers

For us fathers, there are several suggestive and rather upset-ting lessons to be learned from the exploration which provides the background of this discussion. One is that we could get in on some of the admirable and increasingly crucial qualities of nurturing and sensitivity and feeling if we got into the mothering business more. Put off by our biological extraneousness and by the traditional divisions of labor between mothers and fathers, we have left our wives to carry too many of the burdens and collect too many of the benefits involved in the care of children. If the qualities we laud in women are as desirable as we say, we need to give ourselves more of an opportunity to have a more caring character elicited from us by the children we have sired.

Sidney Callahan observes that men seldom experience the opportunity early in life for "growth in self-giving through reflection" that women may gain through the experience of childbearing.[94] This fact could account for whatever validity the claim has that women come to greater wisdom and learn to love better earlier in life.

The point is not that fathers and mothers should function identically in the nurturing of the young. Both for boys and for girls a father's manhood is important. In relation to girls, Dr. Seymour Fisher, a psychologist and professor of psychiatry at the State University of New York, has published some significant findings in his book *The Female Orgasm: Psychology, Physiology, Fantasy.* Fisher's study showed that highly orgasmic women were likely to have been raised by men who were "real fathers." A "real father" was caring and consistently reliable, but also demanding and expectant that the daughter measure up to certain moral standards. Permissive, absent, distant fathers were apt to have low orgasmic daughters, who as women were unable to "let themselves go" with their husbands due to a lack of security. A fear of losing a loved one seemed to underline the low orgasmic woman's subconscious fear of detaching herself from her environment and "letting go." The widespread search for a better orgasm may then be discouraging if it is undertaken through a declaration of independence from men in general or from any one in particular.

Another lesson is that although the future of women's liberation rests primarily with women, fathers have a lot to do with it. Indications are that girls who are willing to be assertive, to take initiative, to be creative, and to break out of the narrow confines of the traditions of women's passivity, intellectual inferiority, and career limitations tend to be girls who have had a close relationship with their fathers.[95] Urie Bronfenbrenner points out that fathers are especially likely to treat the two sexes differently and that extremes of affection and authority both are deleterious.[96] One has to be impressed with the fact that Indira Gandhi's letters from her father while she was still a girl spoke of political affairs with no hint that these were not in her realm of present understanding or future activity. If we fathers neglect our daughters and fail to get close to them, we are evidently foreclosing their futures, and we are prolonging the incarceration of ourselves as well as of women in some traditions and attitudes which should be shucked. As Nancy Chodorow observes, to keep wives completely contained in the parent trap is to force them to experience all their fulfillment vicariously through the children. To leave the rearing to Mom and to fail to provide accessible role models because of our absentee landlordship is to perpetuate our sons' devaluation of femininity inside and outside themselves in order to bolster a masculine identity they are unsure of. Daughters will look down on themselves, and the vicious circle will continue in their children.[97]

Some fathers do not cultivate a close relationship with their daughters from the first because they "wanted a boy." The child of either sex who feels that the parent wanted an offspring of the other sex rather than herself or himself is apt to copy the rejection and become homosexual. As Sidney Callahan points out, homosexuality is a rejection of both the past and the future—both of the heterosexuality which produced the self and of the self's contribution to any future procreation, which is necessarily heterosexual.[98]

Further, it seems that we fathers hold the key to the violent attempts of the male juvenile delinquent to prove his masculinity and the inability of the male homosexual to achieve masculine identity. Five times as many juvenile delinquents are boys as are girls, and their profile seems invariably to include a weak, absent, or demoralized father. They do hypermasculine things to convince someone, especially themselves, that they are men. Violence is much less likely when there is easy identification with a father figure; compulsive masculinity (which may include heterosexual conquest, profanity, and body building as well as gang violence) appears as an attempted repudiation of natural identification with the mother.

Men are well in the majority among homosexuals as well, and again there is usually a hyper-he-man father who was felt to be weak by both mother and son, and a smothering mother attachment evolved. The boy needs a strong father to identify with if he is to achieve a masculine identity. This need does not mean that a supermasculine father who forbids his son to be an artist, cry, or learn to cook is less odious. In fact, there is good reason to believe that the representation of masculinity to a boy solely in football-playing, hairy-chested terms has driven some males toward homosexuality because they felt incapable of fitting the jut-jawed image or unwilling to play a role they did not fit. The strictures in one high school dress code of my acquaintance against hair worn by boys in such a way as to have a "feminine look" reflects the uptight perspective of many adults on behalf of an extreme polarization of the sexes, and the attitude of many young people has been one of active reaction against such views.

Sidney Callahan conjectures:

> Perhaps the high rate of homosexuality in this country reflects an increase in masculine sensitivity and feminine initiative without an increase in the freedom and flexibility of accepted sexual roles. In particular, those male homosexuals who had harsh, brutal fathers (supermasculine) and smothering mothers (superfeminine) would have benefited from parents conditioned to a more complete human ideal.[99]

And Gloria Steinem believes the number of homosexuals will decrease "if women win" the liberation battle for both sexes.

> With fewer over-possessive mothers and fewer fathers who hold up an impossibly cruel or perfectionist idea of manhood, boys will be less likely to be denied or reject their identity as males.[100]

These observations are in no case meant as attacks on homosexuals. Steinem's statement, for instance, follows immediately on an insistence on equal rights for homosexuals. The point is not to make the elimination of homosexuality the focus of societal effort. However, when the defensive romanticism of some homosexual lore is stripped away, one discovers a life which few who are part of it would choose if they felt they really had a choice.

Mothers are of crucial importance in the development of boys and girls, but it appears now, dads, that fathers are more crucial to the healthy sexual development of children of *both* sexes than the mother. Henry Biller, leading researcher in the psychology of fatherhood and teacher at the University of Rhode Island, is one expert who says so,[101] and much of this "footnote" has pointed to that same conclusion. We're a lot more important than we thought we were—a lot more than we probably hoped we were.

3

Man on the Make
and on the Run

Some Alleged Origins of Women's Put-Down

Both J. J. Bachofen in his 1861 analysis of Greek mythology and Erich Fromm in recent years have posited an originally matriarchal society in which women ruled the society and
the religion. In that society the emphasis was on blood ties, ties
to soil, and passive acceptance of natural phenomena. A struggle
supposedly ensued, possibly because man came to realize his part
in procreation, after which men took over and developed a patriarchal order. Characteristics of this order were stress on law (and
legitimate inheritance), hierarchical authority, rational thought,
and efforts to change nature. The historicity of this matriarchy is
doubtful, since anthropologists have not been able to conclude
that women dominated or ruled even those societies which were
matriarchal in matters of descent and inheritance. However,
women have not always and everywhere endured oppressive masculine domination.

The going explanation of male dominance in much women's liberation literature (for example, Millett's *Sexual Politics*) is the economic one which Friedrich Engels contributed to Marxist theory. Private property not only occasioned the fall of man but also the subjugation of women. Millett traces the male corner on the means of power to division of labor by sex and the creation of the family as the property of the head male. Wives and children were part of a male's holdings, and the patriarchal system was guarded by their concept of legitimacy and the imposition of a double standard to the disadvantage of the female.

This economic theory concerning the origins of women's exploitation and the patriarchal social structure is not without validity, but its reliance on a Marxist mythology about the roots of all man's problems is too simple. The reasons for the subjugation of some people by others are too deeply rooted in man's sinful inclinations to be blamed simply on the introduction of property.

The origins of role differentiation in our animal and human ancestors must be traced also to the necessities of hunting for food by some (the stronger) while others (the child bearers) kept the children fed and the home fires burning. After all, nine-tenths of our human story has been that of hunting and food-gathering. The writings of Desmond Morris and others about the growth of pair-bonding (exclusive, heterosexual, permanent pairing off) for the sake of more stable and mutually trustful hunting teams suggest that the realities of survival in a threatening environment must also be considered. We are what we are today in part because men were more muscular and women more tied down to the young. Although we continue to evolve as a race, we need not think that we will quickly erase the cultural heritage which in its origins was based on a genetic distinction.

Economic, biological, and anthropological theories provide partial insights, but there are also deep-seated psychological factors to be reckoned with—factors which get at reasons that have not been nearly so consciously plotted as the push for economic domination or that are not reducible to the hangovers of conditioning from a hunting-gathering era in human cultural evolution.

Fears, anxieties, guilts, and projections are part of the psychological underpinnings of a heritage of masculine suspicions of women
and dehumanizing treatment of them by either degradation or
elevation. Jungian analysis of our efforts to deal with the contrasexual pole (anima or animus) in ourselves points us to unconscious causes of the way women have been perceived and treated,
for which one looks to the depths of the psyche rather than to
divisions of labor.

For Jung, when projections of the unconscious appear which
refer not to one's own sex (as the shadow does) but to the opposite
sex, the source is the animus of a woman and the anima of a man.
These personifications of the unconscious are further from consciousness and less easily recognized than the shadow. The
mother is the source of this projection-making factor for a son,
and the father for a daughter, but the mother image in the son's
unconscious includes not only the mother but the daughter, the
beloved, the heavenly goddess, etc. Every mother or beloved
becomes an embodiment of this image.

Life comes as a gift from the mother, and this memory
creates a feeling of faithlessness when the man deserts his first
love (his mother) to find himself and stand on his own. Not all
the contents of the anima (or animus) are projected in dreams and
visions. This anima appears spontaneously in a personified form
which embodies all the outstanding feminine characteristics. Because she stems from the collective unconscious, this mother
image (which does not substitute for the mother) takes on a
luminous quality and exerts a disconcerting power. Lacking the
education to discern their projections, and content with self-
righteousness, people continue to view members of the opposite
sex in images which are only partly informed by the person in
view. To see that one is striking at oneself when one strikes out
at another involves pain, which people understandably prefer to
avoid. Anima and animus can be realized only through a relation
to the opposite sex, because only in such a relation do the projections become operative.

Jung's suggestions about the sexual opposite in one's unconscious and the baggage we men bring to our view of any particular woman from our own experience with our mothers and also from archetypal projects should at least make us slow to attribute the history of male domination solely to motives as conscious and as pragmatic as some theories would allege. Likewise, such insights inform us that the solutions take longer and require more than economic and political revolutionary measures. A cultural and psychic evolution alone will get at fundamental attitudes, although things like amendments barring discrimination on the basis of sex can't wait for that.

Karen Horney, noted German psychoanalyst, has shed significant light on what she prefers to call the "distrust" rather than the "hatred" between the sexes. Because of our instinct for self-preservation, we are fearful of giving ourselves fully to another and thus of losing ourselves when the partner may not reciprocate fully. We also invest the possible object of our love with such high hopes and secret expectations that the other cannot possibly come up to our overestimation. These are, of course, sources of distrust for both sexes, but she also deals specifically with the male psychology.

Miss Horney posits that man's fear of women is deeply rooted in sex, a theory which is supported by the veneration of older women and the bondage of the dreaded and sexually desired, attractive young women.[1] Primitive tribes have viewed woman as a mysterious being who communicates with spirits and has magic powers which can be used against the male. Fear of her power therefore occasioned subjugation in some instances. Likewise, in the Middle Ages we encounter the adoration of pure, sexless motherliness along with the cruel destruction of sexually seductive women. Castration anxiety is a psychoanalytic way of explaining such reactions.

Man's resentful-appreciative attitude toward motherhood (which can be distinguished from his full appreciation for motherliness as seen in nurture, self-sacrifice, etc.) is also underlined by Horney. She counteracts Freud's "penis envy" theory about women with her own "womb envy" theory about men. Man has admired women's ability to bring forth and nurture new life, but he has also resented it and devalued pregnancy and childbirth in contrast to his own competence. Devaluation of woman to a sex object and inadequate protection of motherhood, especially illegitimate motherhood, are further outgrowths of this resentment. Horney also wonders whether the males' uselessness in the generative process beyond fertilization makes them more sexually dependent on women and thus concerned to keep women dependent on them.

Novelist Norman Mailer, in his *Prisoner of Sex*, supports a variation of the Horney theory when he asserts that men revile women because they have a sense of awe at the woman's seeming to be a step nearer eternity. She is "armed with the power that she brought them forth," and man's desire for sexual union is in part a "desire to drive forward into the seat of creation."[2]

Rosemary Ruether's theory is more inclusive than the Marxist one but shares its stress on man's alienation from nature. It also combines psychological and historical roots in its explanation. For her the emergence of male domination corresponds with "the emergence of the self-conscious, individualized ego."[3] As we saw in Jung's analysis, this ego objectified the world, saw itself as set over against the world, and related itself to the world. No longer encompassed by "mother nature" and thus one with the world, this ego declared its independence, manipulated and ruled its world. In this process it included women as well as land and animals as property. According to Ruether, this ego first came to full expression in Greek civilization. The body-soul and male-female dualisms reveal this alienation.

The root of this dualism lies in a rift in the psyche between the ego and the unconscious, which the ego must constantly struggle to suppress and from which it separates itself. The inner cleavage is projected outward in a subject-object separation. The body is included as object and invested with the qualities of the "lower self."[4] From outside the true self come deluding and tempting attacks on the ego. Sociologically, women and other suppressed groups are clothed with the trappings of the lower self through projection. To them are ascribed the dark, mysterious, irrational, unmanageable forces in the psyche.

Herbert Richardson's explanation is virtually indistinguishable from Ruether's, although he elaborates it somewhat differently. The consciousness of tribal man was mimetic—imitative of the natural environment with which he identified himself. He imitated the biological processes of nature, elevated the mother as life-giver and as ensurer of the life of the tribe through her fertility.[5] This higher status for women has persisted wherever the family has remained coextensive with all other social institutions. (Compare the position of women in the East as opposed to the West.)

The emergence of ego consciousness (from 7000 to 1000 B.C.) and the transition to an urban society brought masculine domination, a partial transcendence of the previous mimetic consciousness, and a projection of it on women. In the city, the institutions of the palace, the temple, and the wall developed apart from the family. Women ceased to be co-eminent; religion ceased to be bi-theistic; law freed man from bondage to nature (to the instinctual consciousness which was identified with women). Creation was no longer tied to the natural—to the sexual union of man and woman. Man the King (not the coequal Father) created and ruled alone, and war became the creator of a supratribal corporate society by its requirement of sacrifice for the larger whole.[6]

This parade of explanations should at least impress us with the complexity of the origins of women's subjugation and subordination. The simplistic male-plot theories just don't hold up under scrutiny if one uses very strong critical glasses. Class warfare theories obscure the significant ways in which the battle of the sexes is in a class by itself. The best explanations won't be the simplest. We are in the presence of a mystery as well as a problem. The madonna-whore split, which is reflected in the iconography of medieval cathedrals with their depictions of woman both as the incarnation of the Vice of Unchastity and as the Perpetually Virginal Mother of God, illustrates an ambivalence which has found expression in every age. The ambivalence roots at least in part in the repulsion-attraction of the perplexing otherness of woman and in the projection on woman of the irrational eros power which man finds unmanageable in himself. Jung would say "projection of the anima." Mystified by menstruation and birth, men have called women unclean. Shamed by their own sexual inadequacies or fears thereof, men have accused women of insatiable lust (and the publications by Masters and Johnson about multiple female orgasms may perpetuate rather than still these insecurities). Tormented by their own fantasies and obsessions, men have charged women with witchcraft and alliances with the devil. Unable to give birth, men have anxiously gone about the business of proving they could be creative by their arts and sciences. Threatened by the possibility of being totally taken in (physically and psychically) by another, men have connected women with death as well as birth, with devouring as well as nurturing. Determined to subdue their own bodies and all that is natural, men have at times instituted asceticism for themselves and pushed it on women. At other times men have attempted to manage their own sexuality by making it a power tool to subdue women, lest they themselves be subdued, and to achieve titanic dominance over the whole created order. Desiring to feel superior, they have found in women a handy "inferior."

Camus, in *The Fall*, explores in depth the need of people to feel *above* others. Jean-Baptiste Clamence asserts that man "needs slaves as he needs fresh air," and that the lowliest finds a way to breathe. "The lowest man in the social scale still has his wife or his child. If he's unmarried, a dog. The essential thing, after all, is being able to get angry with someone who has no right to talk back."[7] From this perspective we are all looking for someone to play bottom dog to our top dog. The vulnerability of women has made them perennial candidates for ego boosters. Of course, women are often used to boost men's pride in less overtly hostile ways than Jean-Baptiste describes.

Richard Gilman writes:

> Men may have sought magnification of their egos through a contrast with women, whom they have therefore kept diminished, but they have also sought in the female an explanation for their own existential unease, a scapegoat for their own guilty pride and a figure on whom to place the burden of their own internal division.[8]

Women have been saddled with the embodiment of virtues men felt incapable of achieving and with vices men felt incapable of overcoming. As the available Scapegoat, the unattainable Ideal, the inscrutable Mystery, the life-giving Earth Mother, the inspiring Muse, the seductive Love Goddess, the angelic Maiden, or the devouring Death Bringer, women have been typed by men so that individual women have often been completely obscured by the images in the minds of their male beholders.

Nature, Sex, and Women—Put Down Together

Perhaps, as Sidney Callahan suggests, because each infant begins life with a woman as its whole world, acceptance or rejection of women, the flesh, and the world have often gone together.[9] The ambivalence we have been describing has produced evaluations of matter, the body, and sex as low or fallen or created by mistake or antagonistic to the spirit or soul, which is trapped in the body. These views have invariably involved the denigration of women even if they were accompanied by veneration of the Virgin Mary.

Although one can speak only in generalities and conjectures, as Rosemary Ruether observes, for the first two millennia of recorded history religious culture reflected the more holistic view of neolithic society. The individual and the community, nature and society, male and female, earth goddess and sky god were not

rent asunder in Babylonian religion, for instance.[10] This carry-
over from tribal society began to break down during the first
millennium B.C. The old religions became private cults of other-
worldly salvation and not celebrations of the renewal of the earth
and society. Nature was seen as alien. Man was no longer at home
in his body or on the earth.

In Greek civilization the body was the prison of the soul, and
salvation meant liberation from the body and the earth to a
changeless, infinite other world. For Plato, Logos was essentially
male, and if the soul succumbed to the body in its first real life,
its next embodiment would be as a woman.[11] Women were
without rights, without participation in public life. True friendship was between males. Homosexual love was frequently exalted
over heterosexual love, although Plato believed that a nonsexual
spiritual relationship between men was the highest of all. The
Greek Pythagoras and the Jewish Ebionites espoused a dualism of
two creative principles—one the good maker of order, light, and
men, and the other the evil maker of chaos, darkness, and women.

The dualism of the Ebionites and of the Essenes was not
characteristic of Judaism, however, and the Hebraic convictions
about the goodness of the created universe and the psychosomatic
unity of man were accompanied by a positive rather than an
ascetic view of sex. To "know" a woman meant a deep psychological union. The erotic passion of the lovers in Song of Songs is
affirmed and celebrated, not viewed with the embarrassment of
the church fathers, who allegorized the book to make it
"spiritual."

Despite these pluses, Hebrew culture is part of the problem
as much as or more than it is of the solution when it comes to
the place of women. Herbert Richardson describes a transition
from matrilineal to patrilineal ordering of sexual and family life
and from biological to legal creativity in Israel which was even
more thorough than the one in Greece, where the principle of
"blood," the principle of ethnic loyalty and reverence for the
Mother, was never totally discarded. There were acute expressions

of male anxiety over women's sexual power. In Israelite ritual law, woman was deemed unclean and filled with dangerous mana, especially at times of menstruation and childbirth. Extreme penalties were dispensed to men who wore women's clothing or were sexually involved with other men. Women were reduced to an inferior status. Wives could not be sold into slavery (though daughters could), but they had no right of divorce or of inheritance. There is some suggestion that man only is created in the image of God (consider the daily prayer in the synagogue "Blessed art Thou, O Lord . . . for not making me a woman"). Wives were treated as property in adultery laws, for instance.[12]

The social foundation of ancient Israelite society was the *Männerbund*—a society of males bound together by common covenant and endurance of an initiatory rite. Whereas the Middle Ages was to reveal a flight from women sexually, but not relationally, in the religious order, ancient Israel retained the sexual contrast and consigned women to an unequal status and a restricted sphere (the family) from which man could maintain an independence. Richardson underlines that in neither case was there the combination of sexual intercourse and friendship—the transition to which our age is heir.[13]

Despite Israel's view of the created order as good, she attributed birth as a nation to the mighty acts of God in delivering her from Egypt and giving her the land of Canaan. In that Canaanite setting the early Israelites came in contact with the religious and cultural forces of an agricultural society which centered on nature rather than history, on the cycle of the seasons rather than the linear working out of God's purpose. Baal, the dominant god of the Canaanite pantheon, was a male god of fertility with a female consort. Baal represented the cosmic male principle and ruled the rains and storms; his consort, the embodiment of the female principle, was the earth mother. It was presumed that the sexual relations between the god and goddess produced fertility, and by imitating their deities the people shared the cosmic acts and contributed to a better crop. These fertility rites included temple prostitution and sacred intercourse.[14]

Biblical scholar John Hayes presents this summary of proba-
ble Israelite involvement and Yahwistic condemnation:

> The Israelites no doubt shared and joined in this Baalistic religion
> and cult. In the popular religion, there may have been very little
> awareness of the vast cleavage separating Baalism with its nature
> and fertility orientation from Yahwism with its exclusive charac-
> ter, its emphasis on historical events as the arena of divine action,
> and its affirmation that Yahweh was no victim of the natural forces
> but one whose purposes the storm and stars could be made to
> serve. Among the militant Yahwists and in times of military strife,
> Yahweh was proclaimed as a zealous god who demanded uncom-
> promising allegiance.[15]

Prophetic attempts to purify Israel's faith against such influences
occasioned a pronounced separation of history and nature, of
redemption and creation, of the spiritual and the sexual.

The Hebrews clung to tribal identity, and they inherited the
kingship and the new year's festival of death and rebirth that
characterized Babylonian religion. However, as we have stated,
the feminine divine role was rejected by Yahwism, and the festival
was severed from its natural base. Natural death and resurrection
gave way to historical wrath and redemption. Feminine imagery
in the cult was repressed. Hopes for renewal in history faded, and
apocalyptic negation of history took over.[16]

The same rebounding effect figured in Christianity's distinction of herself from the temple sex of some Greek cults and the
debauchery of the Romans. The Hebraic view of sex offered the
chance to make it a good gift of God which was neither worshiped
nor negated, neither deified nor denied. It is not surprising
though that the need to insist that sex was not the locus of the
sacred could result in making it utterly mundane if not demonic.
The fertility cults of the ancient Near East were properly rejected
by Judaism and Christianity, but it is also true that, as Penelope
Washbourne suggests, "the loss of contact in both Judaism and
Christianity with the basic insights of nature religions has contributed to the loss of feminine aspects of deity and to the inability to celebrate Nature."[17]

The strictures of Jesus against divorce have already been cited as a boost for woman's equality, and the inclusion of women among his most devoted followers was a public association that would have been beneath the dignity of a rabbi. The story of his merciful statement to the woman taken in adultery and his repudiation of the harsh sanctions of the Mosaic law is one of the most memorable events in the Gospels. Still, he took for granted a patriarchal society, and the lack of any indication that he was married bolstered the ascetic tendencies that became prominent in Christianity.

Despite Paul's view that there is "neither male nor female," the New Testament is still laden with Jewish patriarchalism and the implications of woman's being one with man are scarcely spelled out. Early Christianity saw gains for women, but the Jewish carry-over was joined with the Greek hangover to mitigate against equality for women and also against a fully positive view of sex.

In her article "Mother Earth and the Megamachine," Rosemary Ruether has tellingly analyzed those troubles which were combined in Classical Christianity. The twin culprits were Neoplatonism (with its myth of the soul's flight to heaven) and apocalyptic Judaism. They were both world negating. From their synthesis came a set of dualities we are still trying to overcome. Writes Ruether:

> All the basic dualities—the alienation of the mind from the body; the alienation of the subjective self from the objective world; the subjective retreat of the individual, alienated from the social community; the domination or rejection of nature by spirit—these all have roots in the apocalyptic-Platonic religious heritage of Classical Christianity. But the alienation of the masculine from the feminine is the primary sexual symbolism that sums up all these alienations. The psychic traits of intellectuality, transcendent spirit and autonomous will that were identified with the male left the woman with the contrary traits of bodiliness, sensuality and subjugation.[18]

Despite Christianity's attempts to correct the extremes of body-negating spirituality with the doctrines of creation and incarnation and the covert reinstatement of the virgin-mother goddess, "the dominant spirituality of the fathers of the Church finally accepted the anti-body, anti-feminine view of late antique religious culture."[19] Christianity didn't originate this debased view of nature. It appears rather to have been in the air at that stage in the development of human consciousness. Richardson, we have seen, refers to this shift in terms of the emergence of ego consciousness. Ruether simply expounds this development in terms of the double legacy of Christianity.

The Gnostic heresy which threatened and influenced early Christianity, the Persian-born Manichaean dualism which captured St. Augustine's allegiance for a time before his conversion, and various expressions of asceticism in Eastern and Western Christianity are some of the most flagrant examples of flights from woman, rejections of sex and marriage, and negativity toward things material in the early Christian era. The early church fathers made much of Eve's being the last created and the first fallen. The preeminent early Western father Tertullian called women "the Devil's gateway." Among such Neoplatonistic Alexandrian theologians in the East as Origen, it was believed that the original creation was a purely spiritual, sexless one ("male and female he created them" means that each was both/and, not either/or) and that the subsequent, bodily, gendered creation was a fall.

St. Jerome could only justify marriage because it produced virgins and called women as different from men as a body is from the soul. St. Ignatius likened women to Satan. St. Augustine forsook the Manichaean view of procreation as the ultimate evil, but could only justify the sexual act if it had procreation as its purpose and could only consider this act sinless if it was desireless. He did make the concession of calling pleasure in sex only a venial rather than a mortal sin if experienced in marriage and in procreation-aimed intercourse. Despite his efforts to affirm the goodness of creation, Augustine could not successfully shed the tendency to identify sex and sin in his scheme of inherited guilt or significantly soften the utter opposition between nature and grace. There were even medieval debates about whether women had souls like men.

The development of Mariology during the eleventh and twelfth centuries took place along with two other developments.[20] One was "courtly love" manners; the other was the persecution of witches. Both courtly love and the elevation of Mary can be interpreted as attempts to compensate for the inferior position of women, and it has been frequently alleged that the Marian cult was the direct result of the pervasive ideal of the adored but unattainable woman. Mary Daly sees Mary's elevation as an antidote to Eve's fall, but Herbert Richardson suggests that the elevation of Mary was an attempt to get back a personal conception of God in reaction to the impersonal, rational principle to which the Logos had been reduced in the scholastic blend of Aristotelian thought and Christianity.

The persecution of witches can be called confirmation of the suspicion that the elevation of women in Mariology and courtly love rationalized rather than ameliorated the continuing subjugation of women in general. Witch-hunts would keep women from stepping out of line, declaring their independence, or in any other way getting out of control. Richardson's position is that approaching women as sexual friends and equals in the courtly-love conventions produced great anxiety in men. Fears and suspicions searched for scapegoats. Witch-hunts are certainly not the lone gauge of medieval ambivalence toward women and sex.

The growth of the cult of the Virgin may have been partly to compensate for the past attitudes toward women, but it was an immaculately conceived Virgin who was exalted, and her role as receptacle has been the model of true womanhood in most official Catholic writing to the present. Idealized Motherhood without sex was the ultimate expression of male ambivalence in medieval Christendom, whose premier theologian, Thomas Aquinas, regarded women as "defective and accidental."

Along with the subjugation of sexual drives (and with it the restriction of women) which was prominent in the West in the Middle Ages, one can discern a growing interest in bringing nature under control and an increasing ability to do so. Lynn White, Jr., is one historian who has traced the beginnings of the modern Western scientific and technological revolutions to that period and their impetus to a view of man's relation to nature found in the Judeo-Christian tradition.

Since, he says, "both modern technology and modern science are distinctively *Occidental,*" what was it about the fundamental assumptions of the Latin West which gave it the technological and scientific jump on its "elaborate, sophisticated, and esthetically magnificent sister cultures, Byzantium and Islam"?[21] Why did heavy plows which attacked the land develop only in the West and as early as the late seventh century? Why was man seen as master of his environment, as coercer of his world, preeminently in the West? Because of Christianity's victory over paganism, according to White. What he calls "the greatest psychic revolution in the history of our culture" brought to prominence the "most anthropocentric religion the world has seen."[22] Man now shared God's transcendence of nature and exploited nature not in defiance of the gods but in obedience to the Creator's command to subdue the earth and have dominion over it. Man lived *off* nature, not *with* it like the rest of the world. Trees and streams and hills were no longer inhabited by spirits, as in paganism, and Western voluntarism produced active saints, rather than the contemplatives of Eastern intellectualism. The eventual outcome has been not just mastery of nature but exploitation of it, with ecologic side effects that we are just beginning to realize.

Alan Watts also is convinced that "the Western experiment in changing the face of nature by science and technology has its roots in the political cosmology of Christianity."[23] Christianity is heavily to blame for the alienation from nature and hostility to it in the West which lies behind our fear of feeling and our reluctance to love. In marked contrast is Chinese Taoism, which unites man to nature in an organic whole.

In contrast to the Western view of God as a Creator who acts on nature from "outside" and governs it by law is Eastern Orthodoxy's more incarnational model of creation. Creation is viewed as God's self-emptying. Nature is "not so much governed from without as enlivened from within,"[24] as Watts observes.

Other contrasts between Western and Eastern Christianity are also notable. On the one hand are the masculinization of Western Christendom and the accompanying suspicion of or ambivalence toward the feminine (except for an immaculately conceived Virgin). On the other, there is Eastern Christendom's emphasis on Sophia, the she-soul, the personified Wisdom of the book of Proverbs, its giving greater power to deaconesses, and its lack of insistence on clerical celibacy. Eastern Christianity seems to have been more affirmative about both nature and the feminine. As Rosemary Ruether asserts, the Eastern church defines man not in Augustinian fashion by his fall, but from the perspective of his creation in God's image. Salvation is a restoration, then, not a repudiation of man's nature. There was a presupposition of harmony between the will of God and one's true nature instead of a presupposition of total discontinuity.[25] It is perhaps significant in these connections that Western Christianity has concerned itself more with guilt (which is connected especially with the father through the superego and produces attempts to appease and atone), whereas Eastern Christianity has focused more on death (the fear of which is an intensification of the anxiety of separation from the mother).

It must also be added that along with such correctives to Augustinian pessimism concerning man there was in Eastern Christianity an unfortunately pronounced passivity and acceptance of nature and society. Because little tension was seen between God and the world, there was a tendency toward a static acceptance of the status quo and a lack of the active social change and subjugation of nature which have brought blessings as well as bane in the West.

Why, we might ask, did the consciousness of the Latin

West reflect more the mood of the Yahwistic (J) account of creation with its anthropocentrism rather than that of the priestly (P) account, which, as Frederick Elder indicates in his *Crisis in Eden,* places God at the center and gives nature an intrinsic meaning apart from man?[26] Could there be some connection between the way Genesis was appropriated and internalized and the fact that the formative period of Western culture was, as White recalls, "in the hands of a celibate part of the aristocracy which inevitably slighted the family"—namely, the male clergy?[27] We have seen how the development of ego consciousness was accompanied by the growth of patriarchalism and masculine domination among the Jews, and how the Middle Ages brought the next society to be basically informed by biblical theology. However, another explanation of the mentality White describes is that the Hebraic view of the world had been so colored or tainted by the Greek spirit-matter dualism that matter and sex were put down together.

It is perhaps even more likely that medieval Christianity provided brakes on as well as impetus to the manipulation of nature. Perhaps manipulation became exploitation because of the erosion of an essentially biblical perspective in the face of a man-centered humanistic rationalism which was more Greek than Christian and which came to flower in the Renaissance. The concern to "make history" in the voluntaristic, activistic West has been restrained as well as inspired by the Judeo-Christian tradition where it has penetrated to any depth.

If, as Alan Watts claims, there is a correlation between man's attitude toward nature and man's attitude toward sensuality and women, the question of connection can also be asked about the stubborn strain of Gnosticism in Paul's view of sexuality and the stubborn Manichaeism which infiltrated Christianity through Augustine. Any matter-spirit dualism looks at nature, including man's sexual nature, only as something to be suppressed, controlled, brought to heel. The emphasis on control with regard to sex carried over to nature as a whole.

Even if the Middle Ages was characterized by an attitude of subjugation or control toward nature, women, and sex, there was a residual ambivalence. The cult of the Virgin Mother qualified the kingship of God. Wonder had not yet succumbed to rationalism. The seeds of the technological revolution had been sown, but the harvest was a long way off. The home still had not been pushed from the center of things by the Industrial Revolution. Women, in fact, had power and controlled many industries. Women then were somewhat better off than their classification as inferior by scholastic philosophy might suggest.

Lest medieval Catholicism take the rap unduly alone, it should be noted that the same negative view of sex carried over into the Reformation. Martin Luther, the former monk, did marry Katherine von Bora to give her a place to go (she was leaving the convent and had rejected the husband lined up for her), to please his father, and to spite the Pope, but he regarded coitus as regrettable though necessary. He once observed that women were created with large hips because they should stay home and sit on them. He asserted further, "No dress or garment is less becoming to a woman than a show of intelligence." John Calvin, who did not suffer from the psychological aversions to sex which Luther brought from monasticism, viewed sex more positively than Luther. However, his highest tribute to his wife was that she never interfered with his work, and he valued sex in marriage as a means of procreation and a preventive of sin rather than as a positive form of communion between equals. As Herbert Richardson, among others, observes, it seems to have remained for the spiritualistic-individualistic Protestantism which stems from the Puritans and Quakers to shift the primary purpose of marriage from procreation to sexual communion and personal affection.[28] Sexual union was thus not in need of redemption or legitimation by some higher purpose.

Michael Novak attributes the disintegration of the commonly held sense of reality of the Middle Ages to the rise of capitalism, science and technology, and world exploration. The individual replaced the community as the focus of action. Several symbols (Catholic, Protestant, scientific) replaced the one of medieval Christianity. To use Henry James' pair of concepts, the Dynamo replaced the Virgin (which had been the gentle medieval antidote to aggressiveness, cruelty, and ferocity). Further, in Novak's words, "Reason replaced mystery and sensuality; action replaced passivity; the masculine replaced the feminine."[29]

Karl Stern describes Western civilization after the Middle Ages in this way:

> The theme is one of unfettered open curiosity towards Nature, of an endless trail of victories over those physical forces which used to dominate us; and the negative side of it is a climate of feverish activism, of a restlessness for which there is no stop.[30]

This activism is also a manifestation of the rejection of the feminine—a shying away from receiving or accepting tenderness, a terror of dependence, a flight into work which struggles in deep conflict with a desire to be fed and loved and which is rooted in maternal conflict.[31] Man's active subjection of nature by technological means has, then, theological foundations, but its passage into the extremes of exploitation and feverish activism has psychological roots in what Stern calls the "flight from woman."

We have looked at medieval roots of the Western scientific-technological revolution with its sexual undercurrents, and the stress has been on the exploitation of nature. We turn now to ways in which modern Western philosophy has aided, abetted, and reflected a scientific model of knowing, which in its rationalistic and positivistic forms continues to trouble theological reflection. John Cobb, Jr., has faulted modern philosophy for drawing too sharp a distinction between man and his environment. Descartes, Berkeley, Kant, Hegel, Emerson, and Sartre all failed to grant the subhuman world "a reality such that it can be the object of man's concern."[32] When we turn to Karl Stern we find several of the same names in his detailed psycho-historical documentation of "masculinization of thought" and of the reductionistic rejection of poetic knowledge for scientific knowledge. He traces a Manichaean streak in Descartes, Schopenhauer, Tolstoy, Kierkegaard, Goethe, Hegel, and Sartre, and suggests that "pubescent Manichaeism . . . pervades so much of the nineteenth century, all the way from Nietzsche to Lenin."[33]

Although a contemplative and religious side of Descartes still clung to the intuitive, to faith and the emotive, his thought posited a dualism of mind (a thinking nonspatial something) and matter (a spatial nonpsychic something), of subject and object, which made nature a vast "soul-less machine."[34] He made possible the great strides of the exact sciences, but his method of using radical doubt as the only sure route to knowledge and his mathematicization of all knowledge sounded the death knell of faith for many. Some biographical investigation reveals that Descartes lost his mother when he was little more than one year of age, felt close to a pious nurse, separated the sexual and the spiritual (note his affair with a domestic servant and his purely intellectual relationship with four women, including two princesses), and remained a motherless roving spirit. Similar matter-spirit and subject-object splits have similar biographical roots in the other figures Stern treats.

Having paired the triumph of a scientific model of knowledge and the flight from woman, Stern concludes that "any image of Nature which stops where Science stops is implicitly atheistic" and that the entire subject of Christian Personalism "cannot be considered apart from the charisma of womanhood."[35] For him the Hebrew-Christian tradition should be a cure and not a curse in alleviating the dilemma he describes. He points out, "In the Hebrew-Christian tradition mankind is the Spouse; in the spirit of scientific humanism mankind is an object of experimentation."[36]

On the less philosophical and theological level, the Industrial Revolution of the eighteenth century not only rendered acute man's alienation from nature, it did more to change woman's situation than anything since Christianity prescribed monogamy, nearly proscribed divorce, and provided single women an alternative place of security and greater responsibility in religious orders. The domination of the machine was also to issue in a near reduction of sex to mechanics for many.

The Industrial Revolution had its liberating and its oppressive consequences. Some less affluent women got out of the house and into the ranks of the gainfully employed to a far greater extent than before, but the industrialization also reduced the significance of women's work by taking the center of economic activity out of the home and shop or farm, where women were integral if subordinate parts of things, and moving it into the factory, where the wife was but a duplicate cog in the machine. Patronizing tributes to women delineated women's sphere clearly as that of hearth and home, and "petticoat reformers" of the nineteenth century who protested inhuman mill conditions were called "degraded females" and forsakers of their proper station.

Also in the nineteenth century Victorianism illustrated male ambivalence about women and sex. A façade of propriety seemed to espouse love without sex and make sex unmentionable, on the one hand, but there was rampant prostitution and pornography, on the other. As Alan Watts observes, despite the pretense the atmosphere was sexually charged, even to the furniture with the shapes of legs showing below the ruffles.[37] The erotic preoccupation was there, but it was often given *sub-rosa* satisfaction while marriage was a more restrained relationship. (A similar phenomenon in Southern culture of yesteryear has been documented by John Dollard in his *Caste and Class in a Southern Town*. The belles were relegated to pedestals and often kept at arm's length even in marriage, while sexual initiation before marriage and sexual passion after marriage were often reserved to extracurricular relations on the other side of the tracks with black girls and women.)

Citation of evidences of a male estrangement from nature, sex, and women in the West and of men's own stereotyped reactions to their stereotypes of the feminine is not intended to imply that all has been well on these scores in the East. Whenever the family and tribe have remained more central in a less industrialized society, the importance of women has perhaps been greater. Ruby Leavitt, in "Women in Other Cultures," for instance, shows how women's status has declined where agriculture, women's invention, made the technological jump from the hoe to the plow. She asserts that women's status has stayed high in many non-Western cultures. Examples are cited from the Pueblo Indians, the Dravidians of India, in Africa, Indonesia, and Burma. European primary education has created technological and cultural gaps between the sexes with attendant loss in women's status.[38] Still, one looks in vain for societies where women are fully liberated, and the intrusion of technology and education cannot be delayed indefinitely. Some of the cases made for liberation through sexual communion as practiced in some Eastern religions would put men and women on an equal level, but would virtually obliterate the individuality of each by total absorption of each in the other. This sexual mysticism may be out of this world for some, but it's not apt to take by storm the Westerner who is concerned with expressing rather than erasing his or her individuality.

Violence and Sex and the Post-Victorians

The nineteenth-century misogyny of Schopenhauer and Nietzsche has already been mentioned, but the names of Darwin and Freud should also be added as relegators of femininity to a second class of humanity. Theodore Roszak points out forcefully that overlapping this period of misogyny was a period (the two or three generations which preceded the outbreak of World War I) of exaltation of the glories of warfare and the nobility of that longtime supposed proving ground of masculinity.

Militarism, imperialism, and racism became religions, and social Darwinism and *realpolitik* became ethics as the politics of masculine dominance flourished. Roszak summarizes:

> The period leading up to 1914 reads in the history books like one long drunken stag party where boys from every walk of life and every ideological persuasion goad one another on to ever more bizarre professions of toughness, daring, and counterphobic mania —until at last the boasting turns suicidal and these would-be supermen plunge the whole of Western society into the blood bath of world war. Compulsive masculinity is written all over the political style of the period.[39]

The tale of the violent expressions of male dominance and contempt for women was not over, of course. As Kate Millett points out, militarism became the chief preoccupation from the 1930's into the 1960's, at a time of reasserted male supremacy, and both these developments were aided in Russia and elsewhere by a weakening of the family structure which people were unready to handle. The Nazi ideology is the ultimate expression of the process.

Carl Jung's thought offers an explanation of how Western patriarchal marriage with its polarization (in contrast to polarity) of the sexes contributes to the atmosphere of war and the likelihood of armed conflict. When a woman suppresses her animus, she often becomes dominated by it. She becomes hard and resentful, and withholds warmth and forgiveness. The man's manliness is undermined, and he is often belittled because he does not measure up to her animus image. To assert himself, the man may then act violently toward her, the children, and others. With the patriarchal-matriarchal polarization of the sexes, the man also projects his anima on the woman. She has all the emotionality and tenderness, so he is dependent on her if he is not to lose contact with the feminine completely. His aggression grows as he seeks to reestablish his undermined manliness.[40]

Today the guerrilla style of some groups on the radical left, the he-man pulps, and movies in the Spillane and Fleming tradition with their mix of sadism, sex, and violence are but a few of the continuing expressions of a caricatured masculinization which paired with a female denigration.

If "making war" can reflect one's anxieties about "making sex," insecure "manliness" can also bring efforts to "make sex" instead of to make love—or, more accurately, to make sex because love can't be "made."

If the violence of our age is part of a continuum which includes Victorian times, the sex of today reflects a reversal of Victorian form. Rollo May has described our sexual wilderness as one in which people strive to have sex without falling into love —the reverse of the Victorian love without sex.[41] Fearing the involvement and self-giving of love, people seek a maximum of liberated pleasure with a minimum of entanglement. Hugh Hefner's *Playboy* is charged with making women sex objects to be enjoyed and discarded with the benevolent hope that no one gets hurt. Many feminist attackers of the chauvinism of Hefner's consumer man have become equally wary of permanent entanglements because of the fear that women are inevitably exploited in marriage as well as outside it. So the liberated woman is at times presented as one who gets her pleasure with men, or in some cases with women, but avoids lasting male entanglements—namely, the institution of marriage. Thus from at least two directions there are pulls away from love but not away from sex. However, a few extreme feminist statements are even anti-sex—the reason being that the sexual revolution on male terms has often meant seduction on demand or designation as frigid and not "with it." Man "on the make" but also "on the run" is perhaps creating a new woman in his own image.

A reversal of the Victorian has also taken place in connection with the Masters and Johnson syndrome. As Duane Mehl observed several years ago, the Victorian lady has given way to the "lady of the laboratory."[42] If sex was previously an unmentionable to be shrouded in secrecy, it is now so clinically analyzed that science can give us detailed information about what happens physiologically at orgasm. With the deluge of ink on sexual technique, adequacy, and inadequacy, sex has become a competitive sport in which the athlete seeks to set records, make conquests, rise to new levels of technical performance, and do everything that anyone else has done. Says Rollo May in *Love and Will:*

> One often gets the impression, amid the male's flexing of sexual prowess, that men are in training to become sexual athletes. But what is the great prize of the game? Not only men, but women struggle to prove their sexual power—they too must keep up to the timetable, must show passion, and have the vaunted orgasm. Now it is well accepted in psychotherapeutic circles that, dynamically, the overconcern with potency is generally a compensation for feelings of impotence.
>
> The use of sex to prove potency in all these different realms has led to the increasing emphasis on technical performance. And here we observe another curiously self-defeating pattern. It is that the excessive concern with technical performance in sex is actually correlated with the reduction of sexual feeling.[43]

Sex then becomes a sport not a relationship, a problem not a mystery, a hard science not a creative art. Mastery supercedes mutuality except when mutuality of orgasm is technically desired. Seduction is the game, and pleasure is its name. May describes this current sexual scene as being characterized by a new puritanism which has three manifestations—a state of alienation of the person from the body, a separation between emotion and reason, and the use of the body as a machine.[44] Contemporary man is afflicted with a schizoid malady. He is out of touch, unable to feel, wary of close relationships, more sexually active but less erotic.[45] He's not "animated"—to make a Jungian pun.

What seems to afflict contemporary sexuality could be labeled a departure from or a rejection of what we might call a "feminine" view of sex. Women, at least in the past, have seemingly been less preoccupied with sex and less threatened by it. Ashley Montagu is convinced that "men are possessed by sex, while women possess it."[46] He recalls a study of teen-agers in which twice as many boys as girls admitted thinking of sex a good deal of the time. One can also cite the virtual absence of anxiety-laden sexual humor among women which is common among men and the greater capacity for laughter in sexual involvement in contrast to male intensity.[47]

If women are more able to put sex in its place, less likely to deify it, they also seem less able to depersonalize it. Vance Packard's studies of college students reveal a much lower percentage of women than men (5 percent to 25 percent) who can justify premarital sex otherwise than in the context of an ongoing relationship.[48] Ashley Montagu noted the lack of equivalents to *Playboy* and *Dude* for women. Stanley Kauffmann, in reflecting on an influx of pornographic movies in New York, says that "porno" is made for men if the audience ratios at depicted sex clubs mean anything. He cites Danish film producers as saying that men will work in porno films for half the pay that women demand and sometimes for nothing. He concludes:

> Clearly, far from being universally desired like intercourse, porno is a function of a world dominated by men. Not just the Western world—all cultures. If men lost their political and social and economic dominance, porno would disappear as sexual relations would not.[49]

Certainly social conditioning has a great deal to do with this alleged difference. Some would say *everything* to do with it. Constantina Safilios-Rothschild claims that the evidence from "swinging" couples where attachment is taboo "disproves the myths that women are by nature (in contrast to men) monogamous and that they must be in love in order to enjoy sex."[50] She also cites studies of college students in England, where the double standard was found to obtain less than in other countries studied. Coeds were admitting to "one-night stands" with men they liked but did not love. Desmond Morris, author of *The Naked Ape* and *The Human Zoo*, would counter that there may have been more pair-bonding going on than they realized. As he sees it, casual copulation can only be experienced safely when the pair-bonding mechanism is equally damaged in both partners. The last word on the biology versus culture controversy is elusive, to say the least. Suffice it to say that there is a good deal of evidence to support a "woman's point of view" toward sex and its context in a personal relationship. Socialization may account for the whole of it, but there is more there to be gotten around before the average woman becomes casual about sex.

Women of the World—Write On!

In "The Intelligent Woman's Guide to Sex Manuals," Lillian Roxon contends that the best-selling sex manuals of our time are written by and for men and "within the narrow framework of how men see sexual relationships."[51] The stress is on mechanics; the vocabulary relies heavily on "manipulation," "titillation," and "friction"; and the assumption is that if the technique is right, the ecstasy is inevitable. Concern with passion, feeling, communication, is conspicuous for its absence in the writings of David Reuben and "M" *(The Sensuous Man).* "J" *(The Sensuous Woman)* has an honesty and directness, but even she adopts male values and indulges in the multiple-orgasm male fantasies. "The warm and loving book by the warm and loving woman has yet to be written," according to Roxon.[52]

> Truly sensuous women aren't interested in twenty-seven orgasms; they are interested in a complete union between two minds and two bodies . . . Involvement is a much bigger aphrodisiac than champagne, oysters or a correctly manipulated erogenous zone. Funny, but any woman knows that, and men don't seem to. Just as they don't know in their search for erogenous zones, that the entire body is one big erogenous zone, and the mind is the biggest of the lot.[53]

In a somewhat similar vein Germaine Greer attacks Masters and Johnson's emphasis on the primacy of the clitoris in orgasm and their being biased by heavily middle-class subjects who had a "high voyeurism syndrome."[54]

> Masters and Johnson supplied the blueprint for standard, low-agitation, cool-out monogamy. If women are to avoid this last reduction of their humanity, they must hold out not just for orgasm but for ecstasy.[55]

The masculine malaise in matters sexual is also evident in the literature of sexuality (pornography in its broadest sense or, if you prefer, erotic literature). M. Esther Harding, colleague and student of Jung, analyzes the sexual ages of man in her book *Psychic Energy*. The earliest stages are phallic, and the whole man is conceived in terms of a part—the penis. The intermediate stages expand the image of man to the idealized representation of the whole body (note the difference between the graphic expressions in the phallic imagery of graffiti and those of stylized nude statuary). The advanced stages deal with emotional as well as physical sexuality, and their representations are best done by the film due to the static limitations of painting and sculpture. It is safe to say that pornography seldom functions at this advanced stage.[56]

According to Peter Michelson, pornography has produced the *homo sexualis*. Its two images—the erect phallus and the carnal woman (parodied by Al Capp)—represent the infinitely potent man and the infinitely libidinous woman of sexual fantasy fame. At this most basic or juvenile stage the literature of sexuality titillates orgasmic fantasy but makes no significant attempt to explore any of the psychic and moral depths of man's sexuality as does profound pornography. Michelson says:

> Pornography on its lowest level exploits this rhythm [of expectations and frustrations which marks our sexual lives] by providing easy fantasy gratifications. On its highest level it *explores* this rhythm, its moral and psychic implications, and to the degree that it does this it is poetic.[57]

When literature of sexuality has risen to maturer levels than the phallic, it has tended to rebound between the overly reverential sensuality of D. H. Lawrence's *Women in Love* and the overly cynical black humor of Philip Roth's *Portnoy's Complaint*. The second slant aims at stripping away all the pretensions to holiness, mystery, and galactic consequence with which the first viewpoint bedecked sex. One takes sex too seriously and makes it a savior in itself; the other enables us to laugh at life's sexually related absurdities but stimulates no playful or spontaneous laughter. As R. C. Erickson charged in 1965: "Twentieth century Anglo-Saxon literature is characterized by humorlessness toward sex; indoctrinated by a particular brand of Freudianism, today's Anglo-Saxon writer has no light touch, no really free delight in the sexual act."[58] Incidentally, Erickson feels that John Updike succeeds in "Wife-Wooing" and elsewhere in bringing us a highly recognizable reality which is neither overly reverenced nor merely laughed at. Since then, Updike has said that he attempted in *Couples* to "take coitus out of the closet and off the altar and put it on the continuum of human behavior." Still, though, there is a preoccupation with the documentation of detail in his attempts to show that sex will not save us which would seem to protest too much in the course of the put-down. As Robert Detweiler says, Updike, in *Couples*, has

> *partially succeeded* in doing what no other novelist has accomplished; he has transformed the stuff of pornography—the explicit description of sexual acts—into something like worthy art.[59]

When he contemplates such current hits as *Couples, Myra Breckinridge,* and Willingham's *Providence Island,* critic Melvin Maddocks notes their anti-sexual bent, but observes that "they shudder with an absolute ecstasy of revulsion." He concludes, "What the scene could use is the sanity of a comic perspective. On the subject of sex there seems to be no middle attitude between hushed reverence and ugly jeers."[60]

We shall consider elsewhere why women may be better able to laugh in a positive way at sex, but the point to be noted here is that pornography has been dominantly men's pornography. Women are a series of sex objects; relationship is nonexistent in the game of seduction and conquest; sex and violence go hand in hand. If it has not always been written by men and often geared for men, it has often been written by such female writers as Grace Metalius who have adopted a caricatured masculine orientation with its male mastery and female masochism. If women are more concerned with the quality of relationship and with emotional warmth and less preoccupied with orgasm counting and organ-grinding, we can hope for more profound pornography or erotic literature if more women will turn their attentions to the dynamics of human sexuality in their writing. When better pornography is written, it probably won't be written "like a man."

In "Heavy Combat in the Erogenous Zone," which appeared in *The Village Voice* in 1970, Ingrid Bengis demands "the right to be simply a person, not a collection of erogenous zones." Sex has to do with something all-absorbing—with moving and growing together.

> Sure, she writes, intercourse with someone you liked was great, sure orgasms were great, but in the long run they had less merit per se than the feeling of a warm, mobile body, the whole of it, engaged in being physically close, physically responsive.[61]

One of her assertions is that the English language is inadequate for conveying a "female view" of sexuality. She observes that "all the terms are either clinical or male-power oriented." She discovers that even when she starts using the word *fuck,* she can use it in a number of its popular connotations, but she is unable to use it to refer to sexual intercourse. When she is talking about messing something up or getting a bad shake or telling someone to bug off, the four-letter favorite seems appropriate— but not when she is referring to an act of complete intimacy between two people. She wonders what language will carry the meaning appropriately:

> We have the language Freud gave us—of libido and penis envy; the words Kinsey gave us—of prone position, vaginal orgasm, coitus interruptus; the words Henry Miller gave us—of fucking and coming. Then we have a few poetic words, mostly borrowed from nature, which speak of storms, of quiet seas, whirlpools and whirlwinds. But do any of these express the way a female thinks about sex? And how, in fact, *does* a female think about sex? Is

there really any difference between sexuality and sensuality? Does that difference mean anything? And what about technique? Do you care? Do I care? Does anyone care?[62]

Bengis also points out the lack of female Freuds and Jungs and suggests that more female psychologists might open some eyes about sexuality.

This woman's claim about the English language raises some interesting questions. It does seem that the words used to refer to sexual intercourse convey the sense of something a man does *to* instead of *with* a woman. Is Bengis merely getting at a poverty of understanding of sex which is reflected in our language about it and in turn aggravated by that language? Is she locating a problem which has a solution within the possibilities of the English language? Or is she getting at a problem with all language? Is the medium of language itself inept at capturing the emotional and situational totality which surrounds clinical details of sexual interaction?

Despite its possibilities we have yet to witness a very general advance of the cinema beyond phallic pornography in dealing with sexuality, and there are built-in barriers to such progress. Since the very nature of cinematography makes clinical descriptiveness a constant threat to emotional exploration and presents subjects who are either playing roles or making us voyeurs, Lillian Roxon may be right that music is the best medium for the pornographic message. She claims that the album *The Live Dead* by the Grateful Dead best expresses "everything you always wanted to know about sex and were too cool to ask." The album moves from meditation to tenderness on the first two sides, swells to an earthy, nakedly and joyously sexual third side (which makes it "impossible not to embrace the person you're with"), and then subsides into the weary tranquillity of the final side. She realizes all the Grateful Dead are men, but she believes they understand sexuality as few men do.[63]

When one contemplates the "feminine" concern for personal sex and remembers that celibacy was a male invention reflecting a negativism about sex, a predominantly masculine mentality would appear to be the root of our problem of bypassing people on the way to gratification or conquest. Stern's belief that Christian personalism is tied inextricably to the charisma of womanhood and his assertion that "the sense of the infinite importance of the single individual is rooted in the experience of pregnancy, birth, and nursing"[64] would seem to go too far, but the feminine factor would appear to be essential to staying or becoming human.

We have not insisted that certain qualities or attitudes or ways of being in the world are reserved exclusively for women, but we have contended that something like a feminine profile could be sketched. Whether we are dealing with natural tendencies or with the defense mechanism of an oppressed "minority" group who had best be sensitive, compassionate, nurturing, etc., if they know what's good for them, something we could call the feminine factor has suffered under ultra-masculine domination, to our detriment in the areas of ecology, politics, and sex.

The Late Man's God?

Religion too has been plagued by a lack of attention to what could be called "feminine" attitudes or consciousness. The loss of both a sense of solidarity with the rest of nature and an openness to mystery, which have been identified with the feminine and often illustrated among women, has been a serious theological liability.

Carl Jung and his followers take a back seat to no one in connecting a loss of touch with the religious function of the psyche to a neglect of the feminine. The achievement of the "self" in the Jungian sense is bound up with the experience of otherness. This confrontation with otherness is basic to religion because the way one relates to the otherness in oneself is inseparable from one's relation to God. Since the experience of otherness is tied to the experience of the other sex, our experiences of sexuality and of the sacred are intimately related. The religious function of the psyche is a driving toward relationship or an urge toward union of the personal self with a source of meaning; thus the sexual mode of intense self-giving, which makes for openness to otherness, is seen as the best way to conceive of openness to the penetrating love of God.[65]

Jung came close to equating the religious function of the psyche with the feminine because of the very nature of the feminine modality of consciousness. In its receptivity it does not divorce itself from unconscious processes but adjusts to them.[66] It is accepting, open to the unknown and mysterious, open to penetration by another person or idea, and contemplative.[67] The feminine is concerned with a transforming knowledge, not abstract theory. It expects completion, not alienation, through confrontation with otherness.[68]

In this light, the fact that the feminine side of the sexual polarity is neglected and suppressed takes on critical religious implications, just as the suppression of the feminine in Christian religious symbolism, particularly in Protestantism, has led to further suppression of the feminine in human life.[69] Belief in male divinities in the patriarchal West has occasioned a suppression of the feminine for both men and women. Men inwardly suppress or outwardly project the anima in themselves, and women suppress their femininity by subjecting themselves to an ego-destroying degree to the animus projected on a God-Father. Assertions about the death of God and the utter otherness of God are then susceptible to interpretation in terms of the triumph of the polarization between the feminine and the masculine over the polarity of recognized and related contrasexuality in the self. A woman might see a male God as an utterly alien dominator rather than an immanent presence because of her relation to her animus. A man who has avoided encounter with the anima in himself might deny the ultimate Other—namely, God.

In her article "The Erosion of the Mystery," Irene Marinoff

points out that men have often devised rigorous discipline to get in contact with the Mystery or with God. This active ascetic approach is antithetical to the experience of the woman and the artist. "A Mystery that is approached in so one-sided and at times even psychologically unsound a way gradually becomes suspect."[70]

For Marinoff as for Ulanov, receptivity and cooperation with grace are the essence of the religious attitude and also closely akin to women's approach to relationships. Christianity, which arose in a patriarchal society, has men to thank for the elaboration of her dogmas and the development of her organizational structure.

> However, [men's] touch is less sure when they approach the innermost shrine, the heart-center of the Mystery, the *relatio* with God. Here they are no longer secure in their own world. Men find it far harder than women to "abandon" themselves to Divine inspiration, even only to listen.[71]

Of course, it can be claimed cogently that the greater religiosity of women also reflects a patriarchal structure. One can compare women's greater rate of church attendance and their relationship of dependence and obedience to the nearly always male minister with the heavy percentage of women seeing psychotherapists and the heavy percentage of psychotherapists who are middle-aged married men. In both cases the woman has been sold the line that "the problem" of her unhappiness is her individual problem. Thus religion might be added to Phyllis Chesler's pair of perpetuators of the patriarch-patient relationship, marriage and psychotherapy.[72] All three then would be reenactments of woman's relation to the father and thus based on woman's helplessness and dependence, and would aim at treating a woman's unhappiness as a personal disease which is her fault. Valerie Goldstein's 1960 article "The Human Situation: A Feminine View" would indicate that the predominant conception of sin and redemption in our culture is subject to such a charge against religion.[73] Goldstein's point is that a view of sin as proud self-assertion and of grace as self-sacrifice and obedience reflects male experience and overlooks the fact that women sin more by under-development or negation of the self. The male attack on "sin" tends to reinforce the woman's sin. Masochism is in danger of being mistaken for morality. Her "salvation" is another form of her sickness. An example in support of this outlook is found in an autobiographical account of a "conversion" which was published by "Fascinating Womanhood."

> First, I thought the whole thing was kinda dippy. I mean I liked that it was against Women's Lib. Women's Lib is negative. I can't stand people who are negative—but I didn't want the opposite extreme either. At first, it was really hard to take—that you should always be the follower. And I used to think I should be equal in some ways—but now I don't. I still don't really understand why it's all up to the woman to make the marriage work, but I accept it. We read the Bible a lot. I'm not too religious, but God said it's women's role to be like we're taught, so I guess it is. . . . In school, I wanted to be a marine biologist. [She giggles and gives her daughter a hug.] But I got married. It used to hurt me that I wouldn't be able to use my talents, but not anymore. I still go to college. I may teach, but that's OK. It's a woman's role. Greg doesn't really like me going to school. I think he's a little bit afraid that I'll catch up with him. If it's going to bother him if I continue my education, then I won't, I mean, who am I? I mean it's very important to me, but not that important, know what I mean?[74]

There is also the opposite danger. Germaine Greer all but makes self-sacrifice and masochism the same. Self-sacrifice and endurance are still virtues. Servanthood need not be servility. Self-assertion can and does get vicious. Compassion rates better billing than being labeled a "trap" by one feminist writer.[75] However, when religion does function as an opiate or a security blanket, when it reinforces immaturity instead of freeing people to grow, it deserves the licks it takes.

One can view a feminine feel for matters of the spirit more positively, though. Instead of a self-destructive surrender to the security of a cosmic father figure, religion may find a point of contact in the experience of mothering. Karl Stern claims that every mother is a natural mediatrix of faith, and Ashley Montagu, in describing the maternal "nature" of women, helps explain why. He lacks the anima-animus subtleties of Jung, but he does point up the possible connections between the maternal and the religious.

> There is not the least doubt that women are by nature maternal, that men are not, and that it is the essence of the maternal attitude toward life to be sensitive to the needs of others and to retain the wonder of the miracle of creation and of the miracle of love. Such experiences and such wonderment are generative of the religious spirit.[76]

This sense of wonder as a starting point for religion brings about a much different feel for faith than the Cartesian beginning of radical doubt. As long as men flee from nurture and interdependence, and fear that they will be "taken in," they will miss the head start on faith which a "basic trust" (Erikson) in one's surroundings and a directness of experience give.

Erik Erikson observes that man has often visualized his Ultimate in outer-spatial terms. In other words, the "God in the gaps," which Bonhoeffer replaced with the "Beyond in the midst," has been conceived of as taking up where the conquests of man's knowledge and ingenuity end. An "even more" omnipotent and omniscient Being is predicated "out there." Says Erikson, "The Ultimate, however, may well be found also to reside in the Immediate, which has so largely been the domain of woman and of the inward mind."[77]

The root of several of the evils we have deplored earlier would seem to lie in a deficient doctrine of creation, which is of course a fundamental theological issue. We have noted a Manichaean downgrading of nature and of the material as evil, a Cartesian downgrading of nature as unreal, and a radically anthropocentric downgrading of nature as man's doormat. We might have added a Barthian downgrading of nature as being antithetical to grace. Karl Barth would not admit to any point of contact in man and his world for knowing God. Human nature could not be seen with any accuracy apart from Jesus Christ. He felt that Schleiermacher, Harnack, and the other giants of nineteenth-century theology had reduced knowledge of God to knowledge of man and revelation to religion. Looking within the self at one's feeling of dependence had become the way to understand God. Man's ideas about God, Barth was convinced, afford a hindrance, not a help, in the disclosure of the transcendent God to man. God's Word had to create its own response, and it was a "bolt from the blue." More than one critic has suggested that this stress on the radical otherness or total transcendence of a God (who interferes in creation as a *deus ex machina*) with which Barth launched neo-orthodoxy in the 1920's is at least partly responsible for the death-of-God movement. Barth's revelation positivism was discarded by some for a scientific positivism which demanded empirical verification for all "factual" statements. The question about the existence of God tended to become a scientific problem rather than an existential mystery.

Rosemary Ruether rightly sees Moltmann's theology of hope as a radical expression of the inability to deal with the category of creation which is "typical of modern Protestant theology from Barth onward."[78] Barth's rejection of religion and natural theology, Gogarten's secularization, and Bultmann's stress on the "historicity" of man (which renders him ahistorical) and man's radical transcendence of his world and his past have as their latest ally the radical stress on futurity which sacrifices the creation pole of theology to the eschatalogical one. Ruether writes:

> This means that God is no longer related to the past of the world or man. He is not at the origins of things, but only in their future possibilities which are achieved by ever negating their origins. He is the God of the resurrection of the dead, but not of the origins of present life. He is not the God who created the world we have known, but rather he is the God ever ready to dissolve all that is

and has been in the fiery apocalypse in order to resurrect something radically new in a future world which is wholly discontinuous
with the past.[79]

The roots of this position, she contends, can be traced to
Augustine's complete severance of the connection between nature and grace in his disputes with Pelagius, an Eastern Christian
who wished to stress man's essential goodness rather than his utter
depravity. The Middle Ages, too, we have already learned, contributed to a view of man's transcendence, his dominance of
nature, and thus his ruthless destruction of the pagan's idea of the
sanctity of nature. However, the Barthian and post-Barthian eras
have been continued to provide and escalate theological support
for the anthropology which underlies the secular technologists'
perspective. (Rosemary Ruether gives us a taste of what we have
been missing with the lack of women in theology.)

Sam Keen, in his *Apology for Wonder,* describes a tension
which unfortunately developed into a dichotomy in Judeo-Christian theology between the Wholly Other God, who revealed
himself in the Hebrew-Christian tradition, and the commonplace
secular world, which was considered meaningful and valuable but
not a medium of revelation. This split is seen in "the schizophrenic doctrine of man which is still the basis of popular religious
morality. The body and the sensations, which belong to involvement with the natural and material world rather than to history
. . . are religiously suspect." God has been declared dead due to
his divorce from the common things of life.[80]

In this same vein, Michael Novak describes, in *Ascent of the
Mountain, Flight of the Dove,* a renunciation of matter in suburban America which is symptomatic of the split between body
and mind, between man and the earth, between the spiritual and
the sensual. Coldly rational and willful mechanized man has become separated from biological and agricultural rhythms and even
from the rhythms of his own emotions.[81] Perhaps seeking escape
or meaning through sex, he nonetheless seems unable to put the

spiritual and the sensual back together. Novak sees as the chief task for Western man in our time "to reconcile history to nature, to endure, to converse."[82] The man who has made history by controlling nature is finding to his chagrin that "nature bats last."

Keen also asserts that a hatred of matter, flesh, the erotic, and the givenness of human existence has been apparent in the *homo faber* image of man which has dominated contemporary identity. According to this image, man is both maker and his own major product. Without recourse to some transcendent referent for the source of his dignity, the self-made man must manufacture his own dignity by working, and he becomes the consuming servant of what he makes. According to Keen, *homo faber* is

> so exclusively "masculine" that it makes impossible an apprecia-
> tion of the dignity of more "feminine" modes of perceiving and
> relating to the world; it majors in molding and manipulation and
> neglects accepting and welcoming. Thus, it renders wonder and
> all those attitudes which cluster around it inappropriate.[83]

A Shaky Man's World

In an age which has had trouble distinguishing between problems and mysteries, and in finding a place for the latter in its preoccupation with the former, it may well be that what man has rent asunder by turning mysteries into problems, women may be able to join together by their feel for the mysteries which lie at the heart of life's never completely soluble problems.

Man's penchant for mastery and his uneasiness with mystery have affected a range of areas from the sexual to the theological. It would seem that man's estrangement from nature, from his own body, from sex and women, and from God may be not many problems but one larger predicament into which man on the run and on the make has gotten us.

The need for the feminine factor to come into its own has an even greater imperative than the need for women to find a new self-image which is neither second-class citizenship nor integra-

tion into a masculine scheme of things. The stakes are even higher
than that. As Erik Erikson asserts, male leadership is nearing the
end of its rope with its fondness for what works, for technological
triumph and political hegemony.[84] Lynn White puts it in even
stronger language:

> The world on which we dwell is flying to pieces beneath our feet
> in large part because the centrifugal forces which are more often
> observed as characteristic of men than of women have got out of
> hand: egotistic individualism, creativity, innovation for its own
> sake, abstract construction, quantitative thinking. These are traits
> of mind which, unrestrained by their opposites, become cannibal-
> istic.[85]

McClelland echoes, "One could make a good case for the fact
that the world is suffering from an overdose of masculine assertiveness right now and needs above all a realization of the importance of interdependence in all human affairs."[86]

There are signs of a shift—the sales and box-office draw of
a sentimental book and film like *Love Story,* whose author, Erich
Segal, believes people are more interested in the human heart
than the human groin; the ecological crusade to make us realize
our solidarity with nature; the interest in Eastern religions which
stress solidarity with nature; the various attempts to reaffirm the
body and the importance of touch and body English; the theological concerns with wonder, fantasy, play, and the irrational;
renewed efforts toward a Christian natural theology; the widespread rejection of ultra-masculinity and of violence in the youth
culture; and the movement toward greater involvement of women
in all phases of public life. There seems to be a general reaction
against the usual connotations of "masculinity." Maybe the
"feminine factor" is the wave of the future.

4

Toward a More "Feminine" Future

The Potential Impact of the "Woman's Touch"

In discussing three possible models of social equality, Alice Rossi dubs the pluralist model, which maintains and values differences, a conservative one. It tends to retain a class system and traditional sex role differentiation. She labels the assimilation model a liberal goal which urges minorities to accept the values of the dominant group and melt into them. The hybrid model is the radical one because it rejects the present structure of society and seeks a future that is genuinely new.[1] In terms of our discussion this vision looks to a new breed of men and women in a society which values family, community, and play as much as politics and work, for both sexes.

Instead of adopting a male model of productivity in university faculties for instance, the new women professors may well call into question the now dominant criteria of productive research and publication and turn more attention to the quality of community among faculty and between faculty and students, to better teaching and more service. (A 1970 study by the American Association of University Women included the appalling revelation that as the percentage of women on college and university faculties got lower, the "better" the school. In the four hundred colleges studied, women comprised 22 percent of the faculties and 9 percent of all professorships.)

If Marilyn Bowers is right about a female "capacity to meet the world in a gentler way,"[2] women would then enter the legal and medical professions not simply to join men there in an inflexibly defined set of roles and values, but to bring a new vision of social responsibility to these professions. Perhaps then domestic relations law would not suffer from neglect and corporation law from overemphasis. (James J. White's study reveals that American women lawyers do, in fact, concentrate in trusts and estates, real estate, and domestic relations.)[3] As has happened in Russia, hospitals might take on a different atmosphere with a heavy involvement of women in medicine. Diana Trilling observes that in Solzhenitsyn's *Cancer Ward* the men are still the hospital supervisors, but the large number of women among the doctors "manage to irradiate their grim hospital routines with a sexually distinguishing gentleness and delicacy."[4] (Four of five Russian physicians holding high rank are men, although four of five Russian physicians are women.) In Finland, women doctors were found to average seeing fewer patients and to take longer with each.[5] They also tended to concentrate in pediatrics, pulmonary diseases, psychiatry, and ophthalmology, while men specialized in surgery, internal diseases, obstetrics, and psychology.[6]

In politics the involvement of women should mean not just more "man power," but a reassessment of what kind of power has the most effect and a reassessment of the priorities toward which power is used. Says Rossi,

> . . . it might be that this hybrid model would involve greater change in the role of men than of women, because institutional changes it would require involve a restructuring to bring the world

of jobs and politics closer to the fulfillment of individual human needs for both creativity and fellowship.[7]

On the matter of priorities, Harvard's Dr. Jean Mayer, organizer of the first White House Conference on Food, Nutrition and Health, believes that national and urban politics in general and such particular areas as housing, transportation, and consumer problems are sorely in need of women's "housekeeping" perspective. Care and feeding of vulnerable groups, instead of winning a political game, might become the first priority. The realities of consumer protection for the little man might not so easily be overlooked in arguments over free enterprise and state control. The destruction of neighborhoods might not be as common a side effect of the drive to expedite traffic patterns. Says Mayer, "Let's put women in their place—like, for instance, City Hall."[8] After all, look what women accomplished as the unsung builders of community on the American frontier.

Erikson, speaking from a different orientation, stresses the difference a caretaking input would make ecologically and politically if women begin "to represent publicly what they have always stood for privately in evolution and in history." After a history of war and violence to people as well as nature—brought to us largely through male auspices—caretaking, peacemaking, and nurturing could give a new shape to politics, economics, and technology which would be more inclusive of all mankind, more restrained in the use of power, more conservative of the earth, and more centered on human need. The ethos of conquest and self-aggrandizement has simply run out of world in which to be viable.[9]

Diana Trilling suggests, "Since so far it seems to be impossible for men to mobilize the energies they use for the conquest of other planets for the preservation of life on Earth, women may well have to take over the job."[10] Liberationist Robin Morgan urges that ecological leadership be ceded to women,

whose brains are as tough and clear as any man's but whose bodies are also unavoidably aware of the locked-in relationship between humans and their biosphere—the earth, the tides, the atmosphere, the moon.

In this perhaps surprising assertion of sexual difference, she writes, "Ecology is no big schtick if you're a woman—it's always been there."[11] The new priorities would be of crucial importance. Equal employment and advancement opportunity, equal educational opportunity, greater recognition of the woman's predicament in abortion cases and laws, free and high-quality day-care centers, equality before the law, guaranteed annual income, and equal representation in political decision-making comprise a list which has far-reaching consequences.

Rosemary Ruether believes that women are in a unique position to reconcile two revolutions which at present have greatly differing sets of priorities. These are what Norman Faramelli calls the pre-affluent and post-affluent revolutions. The latter is heavily peopled with alienated "haves" who are seeking new communal, egalitarian life-styles, reconciliation with the body, and ecological living patterns. On the other hand are the insurgent "have nots," the poor and oppressed of the world. The post-affluent group remains, in Ruether's words, "elitist, privatistic, aesthetic and devoid of a profound covenant with the poor and oppressed of the earth." The first group deals in competition, technological domination of nature and people, and group pride, a game which the second group considers played out. Since women are oppressed and subjugated as well as identified with the earth and the body, they could be the "spokesmen for a new humanity arising out of the reconciliation of spirit and body."[12]

Of at least equal importance, though, is the rethinking of the implications of the egalitarian ideal for the political process which some women's groups are doing. It is unlikely that the styles of the ad hoc nonauthoritarian organizations without "leaders" or national organizations could be lifted in toto from certain women's liberation groups and used in the larger areas of urban, state, national, and international politics. There is more necessity and less inevitable evil about institutionalization than many movements will allow as they fire off their needed criticisms of hierarchies and bureaucracies. However, the feminists' rejection of charisma, their use of a disc system to ration time so the loquacious can't monopolize meetings, and the enforcing of rotation of both routine and creative jobs to encourage the greatest development of the greatest number are all embodiments of concerns for greater participation in the decisions which shape one's destiny and for greater limits on elitism.[13] If we are to learn to live in an economy of abundance and outgrow the survival ethic which an economy of scarcity has encouraged, the force of the "feminine" is crucial. And I hope the Yale alumnus who announced at an alumni dinner, "We are all for women, but Yale must produce a thousand male leaders a year," and those who cheered him, are reading this. Just as "cowboy economics" must be superceded in the years ahead by "spaceship ecology," so the male mode of being in the world must receive checking and balancing if the dream of "a family of man" is to approach reality. Germaine Greer puts it this way:

> If women understand by emancipation the adoption of the masculine role then we are lost indeed. If women can supply no counterbalance to the blindness of the male drive the aggressive society will run to its lunatic extremes at ever-escalating speed. Who will safeguard the despised animal faculties of compassion, empathy, innocence and sensuality?[14]

When the emphasis is on continents to be explored, civilizations to be carved out of the wilderness, and scarcities to be dispelled by productivity, man the master and manipulator can legitimately be the pervasive model of creativity. However, with more yin to counterbalance our yang, our technological and political development might have been quite different.

Erikson has said that computers built by women would not have "female logic" but that women might bring a new vision of what to ask and not to ask them and when to trust and not trust them. He asks:

> Do we and can we really know what will happen to science or any other field if and when women are truly represented in it—not by a few glorious exceptions, but in the rank and file of the scientific elite?[15]

Lifton asserts that we can only dimly perceive the ramifications which a recovery of the feminine influence might occasion. The elements of sensuality and nurturance can soften prevailing economic and political approaches to knowledge, and we may regain a feel for nonanalytical modes of thought.[16] For one thing, Lifton looks for help from women, with their better "sense of connection" to the past and the future, for ways of symbolizing death and immortality in relation to the needs of life.[17]

In the arts, male criteria of excellence would be transformed so that it would no longer be true that, as Muriel Castanis puts it, "behind every painter there's a penis."[18] Instead of being considered deficient by masculine standards, women would have an impact far more commensurate with their participation in the arts. It would no longer be a compliment to tell a woman that she "writes like a man." As was noted in the last chapter, the literature of sexuality (pornography broadly understood) is an example of one obvious area in which the "feminine factor" could make a difference in literature.

The Counter-Culture's "Feminine" Tendencies

As was stated at the end of the last chapter, it is already apparent in the younger generation that values and interests closer to those usually called "feminine" are taking shape. As Rossi states:

> They represent an ardent "no" to the image of society projected by the new crop of male technitronic futurists—a machine and consumption-oriented society that rewards technological prowess in a "plasticWasp-9–5america."[19]

From the hair and clothes of the youth we can see that proving one's masculinity is not the hang-up for many that it once was. Rorschach testing under the direction of Dr. Fred Brown at Mt. Sinai Hospital in New York over the last twenty-two years of subjects from sixteen to forty shows an increased blurring of sex roles. Women seem to be growing more aggressive out of frustration with their male-imposed roles and men more passive and noncompetitive out of weariness with the aimless competition in a depersonalized society. Young people especially, he found, have shown such strong blurring inclinations that they have seemingly taken the first step toward "social-sexual reversals."[20]

If the youth culture is tending toward a less sexually polarized and perhaps more feminine direction, there are those who would attribute this trend not to youthful reaction to stereotyped roles and the "masculine" malaises of our time, but to an insidious conditioning of the young by women and feminine men—particularly in the school system. This position is advanced in *The Feminized Male* by Patricia Cayo Sexton, and the author enjoys pointing out the maternal domination of Lee Harvey Oswald and Sirhan Sirhan. Sexton argues that boys who act in a "masculine" way in school are called behavior problems. To succeed is to become docile, passive, "effeminate."

Karl Bednarik, in his book *The Male in Crisis*, is another worrier about the decline of masculinity. In fact, he sees a crisis of eros, of authority, and of activism, and aggression as all being rooted in the masculinity crisis. The homosexual's condition may be a flight from the demands of masculinity, according to him.

It is hard to believe that the male-dominated hierarchies of the public schools are out to feminize boys, though the leanings toward polarization of sexual roles many of them display could create such a backlash. The concern for conformity undermines creativity and initiative in both sexes.

The psychological studies of Keniston, Lipset, and Erikson among others have stressed the identification of the more radical segment of the new college generation with the mother and her values. The absent father, who has been taken over by "the

System" or bought up by it, is perhaps pitied but seldom admired. Competition is suspect, and "love" and "peace" are the cardinal values. Expanded consciousness and transcendental meditation are attractive, and the rat race is rejected. Business vocations are often spurned, and the ameliorative pursuits are sought.

Even if the counter-culture is less sexually polarized and more "feminine," for whatever reasons, it is not completely enlightened about women by a long shot. The study of rock music by Marion Meade ("Rock vs. Women") shows that women are still depicted in belittling ways in the music of the young. Groovy chicks are always available sex objects. Their place is "in between the sheets" (from "Live with Me" by the Rolling Stones in the album *Let It Bleed*). They are often viewed contemptuously as hysterical, whiny, and greedy (Dylan's "Just Like a Woman"). Meade looks in vain in the lyrics for a mature, intelligent woman; only the Beatles' meter maid Rita is capable of holding down a job. In the rock industry itself there have been very few women singers (Janis Joplin, Tina Turner, Laura Nyro, Grace Slick), and since women supposedly can't understand electronics, can't compose sufficiently intense music, and shouldn't play the drums (too weak) or the electric guitar (unfeminine), they are virtually excluded as musicians.[21]

It is also true that the stubborn male chauvinism of several radical political groups has figured in the disillusionment of women with movements for liberation which don't include women's liberation as a central concern. Liberationist Robin Morgan quotes an unnamed revolutionary as saying that "men will make the Revolution—and their chicks," and cites one slogan which promises "Free grass, free food, free women, free acid, free clothes" in its list of available post-revolution commodities. She also asserts that women were labeled "uptight" if they didn't want to be raped at Woodstock or Altamont.[22] Still, there are signs that the new generation is evolving a new consciousness which could be called "more feminine" and "less masculine" as these terms have been culturally conceived.

One of the most widely discussed treatments of the emerging consciousness of the new generation is Charles Reich's *Greening of America*. Reich's position is that Consciousness III should supercede and is now superceding Consciousness I, which refers to the individualism which was appropriate to a frontier and small-village America, and Consciousness II, which refers to the organization-man mentality of the Corporate State which starts with the recognition of interdependence but ends in the "niggerizing" of everyone by a bureaucratic system. Consciousness III rejects the control of people by corporate systems and reasserts the reality of nature and of man's nature. The flowers are pushing through the pavement as individuals get turned on to this new consciousness. This "green revolution" will move from the individual through the culture and only finally to the political system, which will be changed nonviolently at the end, not the beginning, of the revolution. Most Consciousness III people are unaggressive, nonviolent, and uninterested in the political game anyway. We are reminded of the contention of some churchmen that if you can get enough souls saved, enough hearts changed, societal problems will take care of themselves. When everyone becomes Consciousness III, the Corporate State will vanish away. "One does not fight a machine head-on, one pulls out the plug," according to Reich.[23]

Consciousness I and Consciousness II both subordinated man's nature to his role in an economic system; both approved domination of environment by technology; both subordinated man to the state; both saw man as basically antagonistic to his fellowman; both defined existence and progress in material terms and thought in terms of the premises of science. Now a technological culture has begun to produce its own antidote. Solidarity with one's fellows and with all of nature, and expansions of one's own inner capacities, are the true realities which Consciousness III is expressing. People are finding their vocations in what affirms the self, not just in a career. Jobs can become play. Interdependence can be experienced without loss of individuality. The Judeo-Christian ethic can be made a realistic way of life.[24]

Clearly Reich is a naive utopian when it comes to political

reality and a romantic about the counter-culture. The politics aren't going to just take care of themselves, and a nonviolent restraint is not as popular or as certain as he states. Still he provides a conceptual handle for getting at a consciousness which could be called more "feminine," while the consciousness of economic individualism and of corporate bureaucracy has tended to be a masculine mentality (at least, it has developed under male domination) which liberated women would do well to approach with critical care.

Another recent treatment of technology and the cultural revolution is William Braden's *Age of Aquarius.* In his chapter "The Virgin and the Computer" the author plays on the Platonic polarity of eros (female) and logos (male) which Jungian psychology also utilizes. He recalls Henry Adams' designation of two forces—the new force of technology which encountered him in the hall of dynamos at the Paris Exposition and the older force he recognized at Lourdes, the force of the Virgin and of Venus (notice the split). The woman had once been regarded as a goddess because of her force. "She was the animated dynamo; she was reproduction—the greatest and most mysterious of all energies; all she needed was to be fecund."[25] Sex had been strength, but it came to be viewed as sin in the America of 1900. The fig leaves covered Venus, and man turned his attention to mechanics. Women too often followed men in marrying machinery and becoming sexless.

Venus has come to America now, however, according to Braden. He cites the studies of Lipset and Keniston which show identification with mothers' values, and sympathies with the underdog and the oppressed among left-leaning students. On the other hand, one can find father-domination and fear of pity and compassion for the oppressed among conservative youth. The mothers of the radicals were apt to be employed in professional or service roles, such as teaching or social work, where they could actively embody their ideals, and the lack of male models was conspicuous. It can also be documented that the black men who have been challenging America's racial inhumanity came out of mother-dominated homes. Braden is convinced that patriarchal society is eroding and that identification with mother's ideals is not limited to protesters. Roles are blurring and the masculine ideal has had it. It is also the case, as was noted earlier, that Lee Harvey Oswald and Sirhan Sirhan lived under their mothers' shadows, and Philip Roth has introduced us to Portnoy's revenge with his depiction of the Jewish-mother syndrome. The maximization of mamma's influence is not a guarantee of social progress.

Braden also asserts that the computer mentality is being called into question. The computer never has all the facts, and its logic does not exclude madness. The irrationalists fail to recognize the need for reason to control environment, but the technocrats have omitted the element of human values and needs from their manipulations of the environment. Somehow the heart and the head must be united. With many women acting more like men and many men acting more like women, Braden accepts Erikson's contention that there is "a new balance of Male and Female, of Paternal and Maternal" emerging. Perhaps, he suggests, eros and logos are not mutually exclusive, and the values we see being recovered are not matriarchal values but human values. At any rate, the Age of Aquarius which Braden analyzes is the dawning of a future which is more "feminine"—at least as that term has been understood in this discussion.[26]

For the ultimate in repudiation of technology and infatuation with women's connection with the mystery at the heart of things, one can turn to Norman Mailer's *Prisoner of Sex.* He even proposes a sexual argument for the existence of God. Everything else may be absurd, but sex just has to have potential for meaning. Occasionally "heaven may hit your hip," as he puts it. Technology and the tides and rhythms of natural vitality with which women are in closer touch are totally antithetical. So down on technology is Mailer that he opposes any use of contraceptives and believes women should recover a subconscious power they once had to accept or reject pregnancy depending on whether things were right or not. Obviously Mailer is too much.

Dionysus Makes a Comeback

Still another suggestion of a new balancing of the masculine and feminine is found in Sam Keen's juxtaposition of the Apollonian and Dionysian styles. Keen incisively analyzes the pathologies to which each element is susceptible, but he feels that both elements are needed in an adequate philosophy or theology as well as in a healthy person. However, he feels that our time—dominated as it has been by the *homo faber* image—is in need of a recovery of the Dionysian element. The Dionysian way is that of "man-the-dancer responding to the givenness of life in its multiplicity" rather than of "man-the-maker, fabricator, molder and manipulator of environment." The Dionysian is id-dominated, the Apollonian ego-dominated. The latter erects boundaries, gives form, actively orders the material and the mental; the former breaks down boundaries and explores diversity, chaos, vitality. The centrality of will and intellect in the Apollonian gives way to centrality of feeling and sensation in the Dionysian. For man-the-maker, value is created by action; authentic life is aggressive and "masculine." For the dancer, value is to be discovered and wondered at; authentic life is passive, accepting, responding—"feminine."[27]

Numerous current interests such as the return to nature, sensitivity training, transcendental meditation, and media- and drug-induced attempts at consciousness expansion would suggest that the Dionysian way is winning converts from the Apollonians —on weekends for some, but full time for others. Hippie, New Left, and other expressions of the Dionysian way have suffered from incompleteness, just as the Apollonian styles do when they are lived to the exclusion of the counterpart element, and they have succumbed to schizophrenic pathologies at times which can match the paranoiac pathologies of the Apollonian.

If the Apollonian person easily becomes a too atomistic and tightly defined self, the Dionysian can become such an inclusive self as to lack any definition. In *Love's Body*, for instance, Norman O. Brown calls for the end of personality and for a "polymorphously perverse" body. With anxiety and guilt overcome, his brand of Dionysian consciousness would pursue erotic pleasure in a totally eroticized world, no longer obsessed with the genital sexuality to which our culture pushes us from the playful innocence of infantile pan-sexism. Then the world would be the body of the enlightened, all-inclusive man, and all experience would be erotic.

As Sidney Callahan objects, in McLuhanesque categories, Brown reacts to "hot" sex (focused, genital, aggressive) by moving to "cool" sex (pregenital, unfocused, diffused).[28] Since identity and genital sexuality develop together, one has to ask whether retention of identity is not tied to definite genital sexual identification. Is genital sexuality the fall Brown makes it? Is not the attempt to transcend it in "love's body" a utopian denial of finitude and thus of selfhood? How appealing is the regression to pregenital, celibate, oceanic oneness with all matter and sensation which one finds in drug addicts and nature mystics? As Callahan contends, "Norman O. Brown's 'polymorphously perverse' resurrected body is no body at all; man cannot aspire to be a communally dreaming animal."[29]

Keen wisely poses a third alternative—*homo tempestivus*—which strikes a balance between the two elements, each of which leads to madness if worshiped alone.[30] The Dionysian pathology ends in the terror of a totally contingent world and the nothingness of a totally inclusive and diffused self, even as the Apollonian turns the world into a prison and man into a fated victim. Between tight controls and endless possibilities stands the balance of wonder and action, gift and decision, the aesthetic and the scientific, in the "timely" man or woman who knows what time it is in the self's life and in the life of the community and can perceive the world both in aesthetic-religious terms and in scientific-technological terms.[31] Since the Apollonian model has been dominant, Keen is, despite the balance, calling for and in part describing a more "feminine" future for all of us.

The Dionysian way does have its pitfalls. However, its return to prominence offers possibilities for a recovery of feeling and a reunion with one's body. Instead of viewing reason as antithetical to emotion and passion, we need to learn to accept and cooperate with irrational forces which are a part of us without deifying them. Repression (and with it civilization) has certainly not been the utter evil Norman Brown charges. However, Sidney Callahan rightly insists that there are healing powers in our anonymous animal nature and in the unconscious and irrational which our Western rationalism and obsession with control have negated. She writes:

> Man can only reach the heights of humanity by going through his anonymous instinctual nature, not by attempting to climb over or around it or to destroy all vestiges of irrationality. The unconscious, anonymous depths of personality are neither automatically bad nor inevitably good.[32]

Love with a Passion

On the subject of passion, Callahan emphasizes the need for a desire for release to merge with a stronger desire for human intimacy, but she believes that "violent desire and violent release serve to break through the sluggish inertia of man."[33] She sees sexual pleasure as having two levels: the irrational, violent process which delights man with its involuntariness, which "renews the self through escape from control and isolation," and the more relaxed, playful self-giving which lacks the urgent desire of the other level.[34]

In *Love and Will* Rollo May calls for a reunion of sex with eros or passion because there has been a repression of eros after its separation from sex. (May equates sex with Freud's libido and faults the Vienna master's equation of libido with eros.) Eros is a longing, a reaching out, a life-giver (the opposite of Thanatos, the death instinct), a desire, a state of being pulled toward a power that attracts us. It is a drive for union and procreation. Sex, on the other hand, is a need, a stimulus-response rhythm, a drive toward gratification and relaxation, toward tension release.[35]

May is convinced that love cannot grow without passion and that "getting it together" for an apathetic age involves the realization that each kind of love has an element of the other three. Sex (lust), eros (the drive toward procreation, the urge toward higher forms of being), philia (friendship), and agape (devotion to the welfare of the other) should not be rent asunder but joined together.[36] If women tend to be or have been conditioned to be the way we have suggested, they may be more dissatisfied with unerotic sex, which is the symptom of the sexual sickness May keeps citing.

Neither Callahan nor May nor Ulanov can buy the splits between eros and agape which are still being perpetrated by theologians. Herbert Richardson, for instance, makes eros completely discontinuous with love and friendship because eros is preoccupied with orgasm and self-gratification.[37] It seems that he makes the identification of eros with libido that Freud does. He exalts the ability to desire only as a willed act of love in such a way that one is almost left feeling that someone should excite you only after you have decided to love (agape) them. So long as one is not dominated by one's drives and attractions, one wonders whether the total rational control which Richardson advocates in his view of human sexuality is desirable even if it is possible. Learning not to want sex because one's wife or husband is sick, gone, tired, or busy is a lesson of love, but Richardson's case for the "unnaturalness" of sex seems overstated. May asserts that libido, eros, philia, and agape can be united in creative interaction. None of them need be put outside the pale of love, and each influences the other.

Playing for Keeps

One of the recurrent themes in these and other pointers of new directions is the relationship between work and play. Reich's

Consciousness III marks a liberation from a career-defined life which makes vocation a bad word for the majority of adults who hate their work. He insists that many jobs can become playful and erotic experiences. Braden attacks the derivation of man's value from what he produces and asks whether Dionysus is black and Apollo is white, when he contemplates the sense of unity of the black with his body.[38] Keen stresses the spontaneity and playfulness of the dancing Dionysian and observes "the dominance of games at the cost of fun and enjoyment" in the life of *homo faber,* who both works and plays compulsively.[39]

Becoming playful is not easy for *homo faber,* for Consciousness I Man, or for Consciousness II Man. When you have internalized the work ethic as your total life-style, you work at playing, and even sex becomes a competitive sport in which performance is what counts, instead of a joyous recreation in which personal knowledge results. We have already mentioned Rollo May's assertion that people now seem bent on becoming sexual athletes who can match or top others' performances, rather than partners in play. A. H. Maslow says that the sex life of fulfilled people in love at times might be "compared to the games of children and puppies" and that it is frequently cheerful, humorous, and playful.[40] What often happens, though, is that the child's delight and imagination in play is completely submerged under the gamesmanship which centers on "copulation, consumption, and competition."[41] Pleasure rather than communion is the aim. "Foreplay" comes to refer to technique, and fun means producing maximum pleasure (often with a minimum of mutual personal involvement) for the two consumers involved. As May observes, the ideal becomes "sex without love."

The laughter involved is more often that of the dirty joke told to release anxieties, express hostility, or advance seduction rather than the "shared laughter" which has been called "the most fruitful ground for a deepening relationship."[42] Although dirty jokes no doubt can serve harmless functions and even help enable the release of sexual tensions and anxieties, it has been asserted by Dr. Renatus Hartogs that the dirty joke is almost an exclusively male province among adults. Quite apart from cultural sanctions and double standards, Hartogs believes women do not have the psychological need to tell dirty stories that men do. Because of psychological advantages, the mature woman does not need to be bolstered by dirty stories. Hartogs quotes Dr. Martin Grotjahn's *Beyond Laughter:*

> . . . every time the man approaches her sexually, she can show her superiority. She is always ready; he must get ready. She may watch while he must perform. For the man, the sexual act is a test, an examination. If the woman so chooses, she may watch the perform-ance and still perform. The woman is always potentially potent; the man is always potentially impotent. While the woman longs for intercourse, the man performs a kind of "extra course." Where the man discovered love through sex, the woman discovered sex through love.[43]

Dr. Grotjahn's neat distinctions seem too neat. Many women are feeling the performance pressures keenly now and viewing sex as a test. However, it does seem that women may have the best chance to laugh sex into its proper place. Men have tended to put it on the highest altar or in the lowest gutter because they have viewed it with deadly seriousness. Unable to laugh at themselves sexually and to revel in the spontaneous creativity of love play, they have idolized or demonized sex and given it more than its due. That which stumps our efforts at coldly rational control can still be transcended by the laughter which puts it in its place.[44]

Natalie Shainess is a psychiatrist who thinks sex is too primi-tive and basic to be fun; she associates fun with something trivial and casual, and wants to hold out for the seriousness of sex as the ultimate, most primal experience.[45] The play we are speaking of in connection with sex does not mean that sex is trivial, but it is a denial to sex of "ultimacy." Play, laughter, and joy are not antithetical to significance and sacred meaning and passionate involvement. Part of what Shainess perhaps is deploring is the lack of intensity and passion which characterizes "casual" sex as a diversion rather than genuine recreation.

Despite Herbert Richardson's commendation that the

Hefner "Playmates" are sharers of more than sex with their Play-boys (in contrast to the animal-taming model of sex in lower-class men's sex magazines), the sex of the Hefner philosophy is a spectator sport more than an abandoned frolic. In a way each game is the same (and sex is its name), and each Playmate is the same. Desmond Morris' category of self-rewarding game sex in *The Human Zoo* is the shoe that fits. No asymmetrical figures except for the prescribed amount of top-heaviness should creep into the center folds or the Playboy's pad. Having passed the physical, the mate needs to pass the psychological test. She must be eager to enjoy sex with the Playboy but not interested in getting involved and not about to be hurt by being "loved" and left. Can she enjoy sex without love? Can she play without playing for keeps?

Then, of course, comes the performance—the test-driving of the new model. The game plan seems to be the same from week to week, and while variety is extolled, it may be more quantitative than qualitative, and the safety sought in numbers could be a refuge from the threat of making a go of a permanent playground with a permanent playmate with whom one doesn't "play games." Instead, laughter and passion might be combined in noncompetitive recreation.

Since the Playboy is a star in every game, there is no allowance for failure, ineptness, heartbreak, and the other dimmers of sex as mastery. And since the followers of his ideal are not going to be as perfectly cool and accomplished and carefree if they are human beings playing adult games with other human beings, he is probably going to see his unstudded moments as ultimate tragedies rather than comic foibles or laughable illustrations of finitude. Sam Keen writes of the Playboy's existence:

> There is never a hint that upon occasion between the potency and the act "falls the shadow," that sadness may still desire, that hatred and tenderness may be strangely mixed, or that love may sometimes flame when flesh grows cool in age or cold in death. The playboy is perpetually twenty-seven, young but not foolish,

expert in fun and fornication but hardly in love, and hip but not involved. In the image of the playboy the Olympian gods have returned to earth; the enjoyment of wine, women, and song in an alabaster city untouched by human distress has become the vocation of man.[46]

Because of such idealized images and because sex seems to carry with it almost unavoidable intimations of personal communion and sacred meaning for secular man, even if his contacts are only organ-grinding and the meaning is conspicuous for its absence, sex is often invested with religious expectations. When it does not return all the salvation dividends which were hoped for, disillusionment occurs. Liaisons multiply but don't lead to anything lasting; marriages crumble and desperation threatens.

We are well rid of any such idolatry, but if fury is not to replace fervor when man and woman see sex as the source of either their despair or their exploitation, sex and love and laughter must be gotten together. At least in the past, studies have shown that women have a harder time casually separating sex and love than men, and we have suggested that women have often been better able to smile at sex than men because orgasm counts and technical expertise have mattered less to them than the warmth and tenderness and trust of a relationship. It may be that we can acculturate out this "feminine" tendency, but it does seem that women have often humanized men in the meeting of perspectives which are sometimes simplified as "give sex to get love," on the one hand, and "give love to get sex," on the other. The path we are on seems to be the elimination of a double standard by adoption of a masculine mentality for all, when a more "feminine" slant offers the way toward getting it all together—sex and love, play and passion. We may have been making a lot of mistakes raising girls, but we must have been doing something right, too, if we taught them to keep sex and love together. Gloria Steinem once wrote, "the real danger of the contraceptive revolution may be the acceleration of woman's role-change without any corresponding change of man's attitude toward her role."[47] It may also be true that women are fooling themselves if they think they can be casual about sex and not be unhappy with the results.[48]

The union of sex and love and of play and passion in a relationship will, I am convinced, serve as a brake against the current coasting toward serial polygamy, temporary marriage, and total repudiation of marriage. Herbert Gold spoke recently of the "biodegradable marriage, leaving no residue in the land." Alvin Toffler's *Future Shock* presents the "parallel development" theory of love which is endorsed by many marriage counselors, psychologists, and sociologists as a reason for stacking the odds against marital success. He claims that if love is "a product of shared growth," then the odds are stacked against parallel growth even more in our rapidly changing society than in a stagnant society.[49] One answer to that assertion is that agape love, which is unconditionally self-giving, is not an effect of shared growth but a cause. A permanent commitment to love is a permanent commitment to shared growth.

Not only do sex, love, and laughter join better in a permanent relationship, one can also wonder whether they do not grow better in a family than in a couple. Women may have been wrongly saddled with a motherhood myth which reduced their worth and identity to that of parent only. However, it is also true that women have developed a nurturing nature greater than men's because they have in effect been the only parent. Perhaps men have been absentee landlords so much and perpetrators of distinct sex roles so often partly because they have felt so much like fifth wheels in the biological process of birth and nursing. They have often missed having maternal "instincts" elicited from them.

It is ridiculous to deny the possibility of healthy marriage between childless couples or the dangers of a mother's feeling useless and expendable (unless the beauty parlor can keep her alluring) once the nest is empty if she allows the role of parent to be the sum of her identity. However, one can still cringe at the prospects of professional parents who have all the children while most couples do not, and the superiority of communal rearing where parental ties are minimized or diffused has not been proved either.

For better or for worse, the personality style of the children raised in the kibbutzim is quite different from that of the previous generation. Benjamin Spock observes:

> Whereas the older settler from Europe tended to be a philosophical, imaginative, sociable person with strong emotional ties to his relatives, his son or grandson is more apt to become a highly practical, matter-of-fact, and duty-bound citizen, often hard to get to know.[50]

The kibbutznik's sense of solidarity with his peer group is strong, but, as Leighton McCutchen has asserted, the absence of a father figure is reflected in a lack of response to tradition, history, and high culture. Kibbutz children are freer of inner conflict and stay in the middle emotional ranges, but they are more prosaic than poetic, and they lack the highs of ecstatic creativity as well as the desperate, paranoid lows. They are "down to earth," and shun speculation about man, nature, and God. Bruno Bettelheim has called the kibbutz fertile ground for belief in plural peer deities rather than one God.[51]

Even if you like the new product better than the old, there are factors in the kibbutz experiment which probably make it an inconclusive support for some communal child-rearing proposals. In the first place, the level of training and competence of the kibbutz attendants would be difficult to duplicate for all of American society. Secondly, the evenings with parents maintained some sense of identification with parents. Women's liberation groups are rightly urging that the provision of day-care centers of high quality by the government as well as private agencies is a high-priority item. However, it would be ironic indeed if a wholesale shift to group child rearing took place and its result was a generation of docile people who were not minded toward expression of their individuality or insistence on liberation for all. There is some worry that public schools are already doing enough damage along these lines.

The mess many make of parenthood and the cruelties—both physical and mental—which are inflicted on children can make us wish to restrict parenthood to the "qualified." Still, there is a sense in which having children is what qualifies one to have them, and it seems at least to this husband and father that in the familial setting it is easier for adults and children alike to lump sex and love and to laugh and wonder together at the oddities and potentialities of our being male and female. Sex differences can be more funny than traumatic to children who can be secure in the presence of a mature model of each and a mating of the two. And parents can be more cavalier in claiming that they are no longer "growing together" if there are not around them tangible evidences of their coming together with whom they can together grow. Population must be controlled, but let's hope parenthood does not become the exclusive bailiwick of a small, especially trained elite.

Rather, let's hope that the importance of parental influence, particularly in the first three years, will become better understood by garden-variety parents and that one result of the women's liberation movement will be a better informed and educated set of parents who have more to go on in the socialization of the young than trial and error. The studies done by Burton White of Harvard's Pre-School Project on what kind of mothers produce inventive, intellectually curious, outgoing children show that the way a mother treats her child in the preschool years is of vital importance.[52] The "Supermothers" were what made the difference—not by smothering or overly structuring but by casual availability as a resource in the midst of the child's exploration. If the intellectual and social advancement gap occurs so early, how can we be enthusiastic about leaving young children in a collective bus where the driving is left to someone who may be little more than a "zoo keeper"?

If the years ahead are really going to be years of burgeoning leisure, of reaction against the rat race of industrial society, and of continued mobility and rapid change, the family could be the center of activity it once was. It could provide the stability, even with mobility, without which one loses his identity.[53] Someone has already coined "The family that plays together stays together." It could turn out that "where it's at" for all of us will be where the women have been "at" for all these centuries.

What kind of family should it be though? According to Harvey Cox, among others, "The nuclear family today supplies the key link in the transmission of the blight of male superiority from parent to child."[54] He is well aware of the long, successful run of male chauvinism before the industrial revolution spun off the little mobile units we call families. What he asserts, though, is that the isolation and fragmentation of today's world keeps children from growing up in a wider psychological context than what Mom, Dad, and a couple of siblings provide. This phenomenon means that the nuclear family "provides almost the *sole locus* of twig-bending attitude-formation in most American kids."[55] Cox does not see the "one-big-bed commune" as the only alternative to the nuclear family. He proposes instead, as a next reasonable step, Margaret Mead's "cluster family." This cluster is a group of family units living in close proximity but preserving some privacy. The families begin by sharing such things as food buying, cooking, child care, and equipment ownership, and then moving as it is comfortable into additional areas of sharing.

The cluster has real possibilities as an alternative to the hermetically sealed unit on the one hand and the kibbutz on the other, and I am not disposed to make a desperate defense of the nuclear family—certainly not the one Cox describes. However, I cannot buy Cox's claim that there are not in America today situations where neighborliness, interaction, nonacquisitiveness, and the encouragement of intimacy (his descriptions of a conceivable society "in which tiny family units might not pervert people's heads")[56] go along with families which are semi-nuclear, though perhaps not as narrowly nuclear as Cox's stereotype.

Since we live in a small town on a large lot, I am spoiled,

but large contingents of kids are constantly roaming back and forth among several homes in our neighborhood. Games of softball and kick-the-can go on regularly till dark in our backyard. There is spending the night back and forth beyond the immediate neighborhood. Playpens, baby beds, children's clothes, sleeping bags, tools, and baby-sitting pass back and forth between friends and neighbors. Our children see their grandparents often enough to feel at ease with them and have their lives greatly enriched by them. They see great-grandparents and other relatives at least annually and usually more often and have a larger sense of family identification. They think of themselves as part of a church family and a college family. They feel close to friends of ours, who provide them with alternate male and female identity models to balance those of their parents. They see fathers baby-sitting and mothers working or going to school. In all these ways I guess we fail to fit Cox's nuclear caricature, but we don't really pass muster as a cluster either and aren't apt to. In fact, observers would surely say we don't fit any type—certainly not any ideal type. I cringe to think what kind of twig-bending is going on with our daughters, but we aren't what Cox describes.

Most people will want to find their place on the family continuum somewhere between the isolated nuclear unit in an urban apartment building and the hippie farm commune. The family is changing along with everything else, and our places on the continuum are in for some shifts. However, I am not as sure as Cox that the neighborhood has vanished in America or that pulling the plug on the nuclear family will send sexism down the drain. That's another one of those generalizations we talked about earlier. Cox has not advocated the complete destruction of the family which some liberationists have, and thus this parting shot on the family is not addressed to him. However, it seems fitting to conclude this section with Amitai Etzioni's urging that women's liberation seek a new basis for the family—not the end of the institution.

It is easy to declare that "women are entitled to all the orgasms they are capable of" or that, with opportunity for employment secured, they may divorce a man as easily as a man may divorce a woman. But it seems mistaken to assume that out of the destruction of all taboos and a freeing of our biological desires, a wholesome and, indeed, tolerable society and life will arise. From the pursuit of maximum biological satisfactions, there arises first a restless fatigue and then pain. From the destruction of the traditional family comes interpersonal anarchy. It is easy to talk about stabilizing meaningful, voluntary, interpersonal relations, but without some institutionalization, they are difficult to achieve. And while the frequent rotation of partners spells freedom to some, it also spells misery to many others.[57]

She's Black!

Finally, it is worth asking what impact greater input of the "feminine factor" might have on religion and theology. Some implications are obvious already. If what has been said about the death and rebirth of wonder is valid, women's input will be a needed resource in the current attention to what Keen calls the sixth sense and the natural religious sense. If women's views of play can be contrasted with the frequent function of sports as the sublimation of aggression and genital sexuality, women need a greater involvement in the currently evolving theologies of play and fantasy and celebration.

Theologies of sex have had far too little input from women. Women are the ones most affected by theological statements on birth control and abortion; surely they deserve equal time with the long train of male clerics, many of them celibate, who have addressed themselves to these matters. Urging that we listen to women on abortion does not mean that their rights are the only moral issue in question, as some women's liberationists seem to suggest. If abortion simply becomes another method of birth control, we shall have ceased to respect the value of the fetus. Legal compulsion to have unwanted children is not the answer, but moral sensitivity has surrendered to selfishness when inconvenience becomes reason enough for ignoring the claim of the fetus, which is real even if it is not absolute.

For centuries popes and Protestant papas have told women about their true nature. Marilyn Bowers observes:

> Even attempts at a theology of woman have been detrimental because they assume from the start the importance of sexual differentiation over and above personhood. Studies on man most often begin with his humanness while those of women begin with sex.[58]

The polarity of human sexuality does, however, offer possibilities in ongoing discussion about what if anything in human experience can serve as a starting point for talk about God. Ulanov's exploration of Jungian psychology suggests that our earliest encounter with "otherness" has unavoidably sexual connotations and that man's and woman's sexuality is inextricably tied up with their relationship to God. The image of God in us, then, is tied with contrasexuality. Working this plot does not mean that the search for God and for a better orgasm are the same thing and that you can't know God if you haven't "known" a member of the opposite sex in physical intercourse. In our biblical heritage, though, there was such an awareness of the abuses of the nature religions with their fertility cults that sexuality became too suspect to qualify as humanity's preparation to meet God.

Mary Daly believes that the search for new theological concepts and images of a less masculine bent might see a greater emphasis on other descriptions of human sin than the often dominant diagnosis as offense against those in power.[59] We have already cited Valerie Goldstein's contention that woman's particular temptation is the underdevelopment of the self and her particular sin the refusal to take responsibility. Current concerns with apathy (Cox) and emptiness (Erikson), fundamental human ailments, suggest more "feminine" correctives to the Promethean model of rebellion and defiance.

Robert Lifton's contention that women's greater sense of

connection could provide better ways of symbolizing death and immortality suggests another respect in which theology has a lot of unfinished business and women theologians may have a lot of unused capital to offer. Perhaps for them the "womb of death" can be viewed as the context of a new birth and not as the ultimate devourer of personal identity. Contemporary man's veneering death with euphemisms and cosmetics indicates that it is one mystery he still holds in awe. Despite freezing and organ transplants, death will not be reduced to a problem. Rollo May calls death the new pornography—the unmentionable—and sees preoccupation with sex as an escape from facing death.[60]

Mention also has been made of the black theologies of liberation and revolution. If the church in the gospel tradition must "think black" or forsake its calling, the church must also "think broadly" if it is really concerned with the liberation of people from all that enslaves them and does violence to their humanity. The stories about the man who had seen God and came back to report "She's black" and about the jailed suffragettes who prayed to God hoping that "She" would deliver them get to the heart of the matter. If the black consciousness can legitimately be fed on the Exodus of Israel and the exorcisms of Jesus, so too can the feminist consciousness. If the Shrine of the Black Madonna can sing "Darkest Lord Jesus," we can surely think in more feminine terms about Jesus without claiming that he was homosexual. We can leave to others the assertions that Jesus would have been a great football player if he had lived in our time.

Esther Woo of Fordham University has even suggested a shift of the Trinitarian reference to "Mother, Daughter and Holy Spirit" as a reaction against male images of God and the church's perpetuation of a male-dominated society based on a male incarnation. It is Woo's conviction that there would be more trust in prayer if God were our Mother.[61] We need not follow Jung's suggestion that the Trinity should become the Quadrinity, to include the feminine principle.[62] The motherhood of God has possibilities, and the Wise Woman archetype may shed some light on the Sophia figure depicted in the Bible's Wisdom tradition as present with God at creation. The Holy Spirit could do with some designations as "she," and "her" sanctifying work can be illuminated by Jungian understanding of the religious function of the psyche, which is closely connected to the feminine.

Our liturgies need pronouns of both genders, and we should encourage women to get busy with prayers that not only view God in more varied ways than as a father figure but also express human need in ways with which women can better identify. I doubt that Jesus would say that we had turned our backs on his teaching if on occasion we prayed, "Our Mother, in whom our earth and we live and move, sacred is your name. May your family be gathered and your love be returned in the measure in which it has been poured forth. Nourish and nurture us today. Receive us to yourself despite our estrangement, that we may be empowered to receive others to ourselves despite their estrangement from us. Do not forsake or smother us, for in you we trust." Of course, American momism and lack of "animation" among men present barriers, and the Mother is not the only feminine archetype to be explored. We should not assume that mere shifts in pronouns will produce a genuine transformation in our understanding of God.

An interest in theology which deserves special mention with reference to women is process theology, which attempts to appropriate the philosophies of Alfred North Whitehead and Charles Hartshorne for Christian thought. We have pinpointed earlier the complicity of an inadequate doctrine of creation in some of the theological evils we have been deploring and the need to reunite nature and history. The demise of Mother Earth aided the rise of the Megamachine, to use Rosemary Ruether's terms. Such theologians as John Cobb, Jr., Schubert Ogden, Daniel Day Williams, and Norman Pittenger have been attempting to get at some of these problems by way of process philosophy. They are concerned to make much of creation without forgetting redemption, to work out a Christian natural theology, and to work out the implications of saying God is love for understanding his power.

The process position emphasizes the dynamism and relational character of all life and the unity of man with nature and of nature with God. Polarity between the abstract and fixed and the relational is part of each individual life—including God's. There is both an abstract eternal being of God and a dynamic social aspect—a di-polarity—which enables the rejection of pantheism (nature is God) and the affirmation of panentheism (nature is part of God, or "the world is God's body" [Hartshorne]). God's creativity, love, suffering are understood in terms of an interaction between God and the world, which means that God is affected by the world and that God as receptacle preserves all value. "He" inspires or lures or attracts the process of creative advance, but he does not dictate or manipulate. His power is the power of persuasion rather than of predestination.

Penelope Washbourne sees the possibility of using the term "feminine" for this feeling and responding aspect of God. She suggests the appropriateness of a very feminine metaphor for God's creativity which harmonizes with Eastern Christianity's view of creation as God's self-emptying and of nature as enlivened from within, not governed from without.

> How much better for theology to conceive of God the Creator as pregnant with the world, giving birth to it and nourishing it, than of God the divine Watchmaker who set the machine ticking millions of years ago.[63]

Since the latter is the conception of God the Creator that natural religion came to espouse during the Enlightenment in Europe and the rise of rationalistic deism in England, it is not surprising that Schleiermacher focused on a feeling of absolute dependence and the immanence of God, in contrast to Kant's religion within the limits of reason alone and his remote Lawgiver God. (Barth's reaction to Schleiermacher then can be seen as a "masculine" reaction to Schleiermacher's "feminine" reaction.)

Washbourne also suggests that the Spirit as part of God be

understood not so much in terms of rationality and structure but as "a principle of creativity and novelty" more in keeping with the feminine Wisdom of the Old Testament. If the feminine can be identified with such an inbreaking and disruptive force in God, then the ordering masculine aspect can be understood as Logos.[64]

She seems to be in harmony with Sam Keen's treatment of the Apollonian and Dionysian elements with this attempt to draw theology away from exclusive ties to the logical, abstract, ordered, and static understandings of God toward the more affective, concrete, disordering, and dynamic pole. Keen sets up his polarity this way:

The Apollonian Way	*The Dionysian Way*
Theism or deism. God is a being encountered as a Thou, revealing himself in unique acts in history	Pantheism or Panentheism. God is being itself, the encompassing, the power of being in all, known in the density of experiences in which value is discovered.
A theology of the Word, work, action, speaking, willing, thinking, consciousness, order.	A theology of the spirit, leisure, play, listening, waiting, feeling, chaos, the unconscious.[65]

Neither Keen nor Washbourne would swap a masculine theology wholly for a feminine one. The Schleiermachers and Tillichs need to be balanced with the Barths and the Moltmanns. The pendulum just needs and seems to be getting a "feminine" swing with so much masculinity to counterbalance. Women like Professor Washbourne will hopefully be real swingers in this ongoing process. She writes, "God is both feminine and masculine, mother and father, who finds fullest expression in the meeting of egg and sperm, the creation of life itself."[66]

Another way to get at what we are saying is through an

understanding of God as love. As Norman Pittenger observes, theism has often made God so independent and absolute that he (she?) seemed more indifferent than loving.[67] Process theology attempts to present sharing, participation, change, giving, and receiving as the very nature of God. God's omnipresence means cosmic love is everywhere active; God's omnipotence means love is indefatigable and ultimately convincing though not coercive; God's omniscience refers to love's awareness of and sensitivity to all possible opportunities and occasions for loving. Evil may resist the lure of love, but all that is good is kept by God, "the fellow-sufferer who understands."[68] Love ultimately wins through a compelling which does not destroy freedom. As John Cobb states, compulsion can be exercised only on the powerless; "persuasion is the means of exercising power upon the powerful."[69]

Women just may have some better insights into power so understood than men, since women's power has usually been the persuasiveness of those who could not dictate. The power of parent over child is a much better analogy to the power of God than that of a hammer over a nail or a potter over clay. Further, the usual idea of a father's absolute and unwavering authority needs to give way to that of a mother's flexible and supportive authority, which is aimed toward development more than dominance.[70] As Whitehead points out, the church gave God the attributes which belonged to Caesar—the coercive power of imperial rule—when the Western world accepted Christianity. Three strands of thought emerged in the formative period of theistic philosophy. God as imperial ruler (associated with the divine Caesars), God as personification of moral energy (Hebrew prophets), and God as unmoved mover (Aristotle).[71] In its origins, Whitehead feels, Christianity had another, better suggestion than any of these stands:

> It dwells upon the tender elements in the world, which slowly and in quietness operate by love; and it finds purpose in the present immediacy of a kingdom not of this world. Love neither rules, nor

is it unmoved; also it is a little oblivious as to morals. It does not look to the future; for it finds its own reward in the immediate present.[72]

This glimpse of Whitehead's thought is a good indication of why process philosophy is seen as a rich resource for a more "feminine" theology.

Another way in which man's estrangement from nature and God's separation from it are being challenged is through what some call eco-theology. If the Christian tradition has contributed to the exploitation of nature, as Lynn White, Alan Watts, Harvey Cox, and others have suggested, there are those who believe it can also enable a recovery of a sense of solidarity with nature which the ecological crusade is emphasizing. If, as Rosemary Ruether contends, the ditching of the legacy of Mother Earth contributed to the technological ravishing by the "megamachine," the patriarchal polarization of Western thought needs all the help it can get to become "de-dualized." According to White, "What we do about ecology depends on our ideas of the man-nature relationship. More science and more technology are not going to get us out of the present ecologic crisis until we find a new religion, or rethink our old one."[73] He does not think that Zen Buddhism or other Eastern religious proponents of man's union with nature are really viable options for Western man but suggests that St. Francis of Assisi become the patron saint of a more ecology-conscious Christianity which sees the animal, vegetable, and mineral environment in a more brotherly and sisterly way. A democracy of God's creatures needs to replace man's monarchy. It should be admitted, though, that St. Francis had his own problems regarding matter, the human body, and sex, even if he did feel related to animals and heavenly bodies in a familial way.

A growing body of theological writing is concerned with making a habitable home out of the earth and with balancing what Harvey Cox calls "planned acquiescence" with the central mentality of the technologist. As we come to have a more inner-spatial, housekeeping sense of our environment, Erikson's "feminine" spatial consciousness should inform our environmental theology and ethics.

The attraction of Eastern religions for the young has been attributable in part to their rejection of aggressive, autonomous individualism in favor of the passive merger of the self into the social and cosmic whole and their sense of man's living with nature rather than off nature. Unlike Lynn White, Alan Watts thinks Zen Buddhism is right for the West, with its differing view of the nature, man, and God relationship. However, the loss of self which is entailed in the way of Zen, as illustrated, for instance, in the fusion of the sexual mysticism Watts describes, is not apt to satisfy the Western man who has sought to find rather than lose his identity. Nor is it apt to convert the Christian man whose belief in the resurrection of the body affirms the preservation of the self, not the loss of it, and whose view of social relationships —sexual and otherwise—is one of individuality in community or communion. Even process thought is unsatisfactory for some on the score of personal identity. Zen's passive receptivity and the rendering of evil and moral choice as illusory and irrelevant are also not apt to pass muster with a more activistic and voluntaristic and "masculine" orientation.

Christianity needs to become more "feminine," but not to forsake the "masculine" orientation as entirely as the way of Zen would. Zen does challenge the Christian tradition to mend its "feminine" fences though.

The contribution of women and attention to "the feminine" should enrich theology in many of its areas, not just such specific themes or subjects as these. And what is more, male theologians would do well to remember that those books they hope the theologically literate laymen will read are by and large bought and read by the much larger number of theologically literate laywomen who make up the backbone of the church even when they take a back seat.

Quite apart from a greater infiltration by women of the

ranks of the churches' professional theologians, the faith and practice of the Christian community will surely be affected significantly if and when women are accorded authority and power commensurate with their numbers and involvement. Roman Catholic priest-sociologist Joseph H. Fichter has said concerning his own communion that "we shall witness the complete removal of discrimination in the Catholic church on the day when there is a pregnant Pope who is either African or Asiatic."[74] This development would, of course, be more than a token gesture toward women such as election of one as president or moderator of a Protestant communion. It would involve allowing women clergy as well as married clergy, plus support among the cardinals for election to a permanent, not temporary, position as ruler, not simply as presiding officer. What the Protestant equivalent would be would depend on the form of government of the body. In addition to the freshness which new blood would bring to the perspective of church leadership, there just might be some new priorities in the works. The men who withdraw from active involvement because women get their due are expendable no matter how many they are. If they knew what the church is, they wouldn't leave, and there is no longer any excuse for electing a man elder or deacon because his wife has been a valuable and dedicated member of the church.

What should be sought, of course, is neither a "masculine" nor a "feminine" church but a human church in which both sexes are recognized first as children of God and only secondarily as men or women. If the correction of "masculine" domination of the church were to be "feminine" domination, the balance which should be struck between these two factors in human life would be lost. There is a present need, though, to make an extra effort to swing the balance in the women's direction.

And a Twist of Tom Harris for Topping

What is needed in the individual self, in the family, in the church, in the university or college, and in the larger society is the complement of one factor by the other. In our concern for a recovery of the feminine factor we have said that on numerous fronts the stakes are high and that the masculine factor is "better wed than dead," quite apart from the liberation women deserve. However, a more "feminine" future should not mean an "unmasculine" future. The polarized stereotypes of femininity and masculinity will be good riddance, but, in Thomas Harris' terms, the "OK-ness" of both masculine and feminine needs to be affirmed both in the self and in social relations. In fact, Harris' four life positions in *I'm OK—You're OK* make useful ways to analyze both the problems and the solution we have been considering.

"I'm not OK—you're OK" describes the anxious dependency of the immature. Endemic to the early experience of the child, this phrase aptly describes the plight of the patronized, babied female who learns to regard herself as the second sex because her male-dominated culture communicates this evaluation to her with countless stimuli. "Fascinating Womanhood" is a dead ringer for this position. With respect to the person, this position describes those men whose anima has taken them over often as a projection on the mother or another woman and those women who have so identified with the animus that they have completely swapped the feminine for the masculine. This position could be used to describe many persons who are homosexual.

"I'm not OK—you're not OK" is the desperate utterance of the subjugated who have seen the clay feet on the inside of the master's boot. Perhaps we can use this position to catch the mood of the woman who knows she's got it bad, but has not gained a new self-image. It describes those who have turned on the opposite sex, but do not really believe in the goodness of their own. The self-conscious anti-femininity of the "Bitch Manifesto," which goes out of its way to flaunt usual feminine characteristics, could be Exhibit A here. In the person, this phrase affords a profile of a person who has not faced up to the contrasexual pole in the self and who also has repudiated his or her basic biological sexuality.

"I'm OK—you're not OK" goes along with screams of

"male chauvinist pig" by female-elevating, male-denigrating women and parallel epithets by defensive males who challenge or respond in kind. Still uneasy about my worth, I attempt to bolster my stature by blasting another's. The newly liberated woman who has just recovered or discovered pride in her femaleness would fit this position.

In the self, this position points up the polarized sexuality of the person who seeks to affirm his or her fundamental sexual identity by shunting or repressing the anima or animus—perhaps projecting it on members of the opposite sex and relating with hostility to them.

The position the sexes can hopefully assume both within the self and in relation to each other individually is "I'm OK— you're OK." This way neither sex is compelled to fulfill "ifs" for acceptance. Traditional masculine and feminine stereotypes would not be imposed on others or on oneself. Nor would either assume that the only way to be fully human would be to shuck the sexual identity which the body indicates and to become the other sex where the grass looks greener and the constricting societal role definitions of one's own sex can be left behind. Rather, men and women could affirm the goodness of their own and each other's sexuality and free each other to realize their humanity. Their humanity could continue to differ but not according to fixed definitions or rigidly divided compartments of difference. When one feels valued as one is, there is no necessity for sex-role posturing nor for rejecting the goodness of our being females or males.

The intrapersonal condition which reflects such a position is the one in which the anima or animus has been faced and included in a dynamic polar selfhood. Affirmation of his anima changes the man's view both of himself and of women. The same is true for a woman and her animus. The movement between the personal and the social goes both ways. One's relationship to members of the opposite sex affects deeply the health or sickness of one's view of the contrasexual pole in himself, and the self's relation to its anima or animus will dictate the nature of one's relationship to persons of the opposite sex. We can work at it from both ends. A new personal understanding, acceptance, and gratitude with respect to the intrapersonal polarity will make us less sexist members of society; less sexist structures in society will enable us to think differently about the otherness in ourselves.

As we know only too well, it takes more than a new year's resolution to believe in our OK-ness or the OK-ness of others. To affirm the goodness of another's being, including her or his sexuality, we must feel that we are valued, that our sexuality, including the contrasexuality in us, is good. Having been affirmed, accepted, loved, we are enabled to affirm, accept, love. In this connection the Christian church talks about the grace of God—his (her) affirmation of our value and his loving us into loving. This liberating prevenient grace does not come to us in a void. If no people have ever affirmed and accepted us, we can hardly believe God does. And if human love is so crucial, the person who does not believe in God can justifiably ask why we claim the need for the grace of God. There is no airtight answer, but faith asserts that human love slips into attaching "ifs" to its acceptance as well as into outright rejection and that ultimately one's own value and that of the neighbor is founded in the valuing, and accepting, of a transcendent Creator and Redeemer. In expressing such a faith, we need not, in fact, should not, contend that "our way" is the only way lives ever get so graced. We may believe that the atheist who affirms that he and his neighbor are both OK has been "graced" by God, but he would be hard to convince of that. We can say, though, that saying OK is not easy and that unless we've been OK'd, we can't.

Like the OK-OK self, the OK-OK society is not an easy progression from what has gone before it. It is taking a revolution to usher in such a society, but the revolution will be more apparent than real if it only brings a different balance of power with no change in our uses of power. If women break down doors to professional, political, and ecclesiastical spheres which have been closed to them, they will have gotten their due, but we will still have "business as usual." We don't just need different people wearing different hats. We need to "flip our lids." What's at stake is the liberated humanity of us all. One of the most memorable posters to come out of the protests against the war in Vietnam asks, "What if they gave a war and nobody came?" Now, it seems, we should ask ourselves, "What if they gave a revolution and everybody won?"

Notes

A Straightforward Foreword

1. Daniel C. Maguire, "Realepistemologie Confronts Realpolitik," in *"Story" in Politics*, by Michael Novak and others (New York: The Council on Religion and International Affairs, 1970), pp. 81–82.

1. Blacks and Broads

1. Theodore Roszak, "The Hard and the Soft: The Force of Feminism in Modern Times," in *Masculine/Feminine: Readings in Sexual Mythology and the Liberation of Women*, ed. Betty Roszak and Theodore Roszak (New York: Harper & Row, 1969), p. 99.

2. Helen Mayer Hacker, "Women as a Minority Group," in *Masculine/Feminine*, pp. 140–141. Reprinted from *Social Forces*, October 1951. Used by permission of the University of North Carolina Press.

3. Summarized in Catharine Stimpson, " 'Thy Neighbor's Wife, Thy Neighbor's Servants': Women's Liberation and Black Civil Rights," in *Woman in Sexist Society: Studies in Power and Powerlessness*, ed. Vivian Gornick and Barbara K. Moran (New York: Basic Books, 1971), p. 473.

4. Susan Kennedy Calhoun, "Women in the Professional Schools," *Yale Alumni Magazine*, Vol. 32, No. 7 (April 1970), p. 44.

5. Saul Bellow, *Mr. Sammler's Planet* (New York: Viking Press, 1970), pp. 206–207.

6. Thomas W. Ogletree, "The Gospel as Power: Explorations in a Theology of Social Change," in *New Theology No. 8*, ed. Martin E. Marty and Dean G. Peerman (New York: The Macmillan Co., 1971), p. 187.

7. Dorothy Sayers, "The Human-Not-Quite-Human," in *Mas-*

culine/Feminine, pp. 121–122. Reprinted from *Unpopular Opinions*. Used by permission of Fernhill House, Ltd.

8. Quoted in Marlene Dixon, "The Rise of Women's Liberation," in *Masculine/Feminine*, p. 201.

9. Germaine Greer, *The Female Eunuch* (New York: McGraw-Hill Book Co., 1970), p. 299.

10. Robin Morgan, "Goodbye to All That," in *Masculine/Feminine*, p. 243.

11. George D. Colman, "Racism: New Alternatives for Management," *Life and Work* (a publication of the Detroit Industrial Mission), Vol. 13, No. 1 (Spring 1971). See also Robert W. Terry, *For Whites Only* (Grand Rapids: Wm. B. Eerdmans, 1970).

12. Joreen, "The Bitch Manifesto," in *Masculine/Feminine*, pp. 275–276.

13. An inference of equal opportunity for blacks from such Christian principles as universality and personal uniqueness is drawn in detailed fashion by Joseph C. Hough, Jr., *Black Power and White Protestants* (New York: Oxford University Press, 1968), pp. 153–160.

14. Greer, p. 303.

15. Stimpson, pp. 473–474.

16. Norman Faramelli, "Ecological Responsibility and Economic Justice," in *Ecology: Crisis and New Vision*, ed. Richard E. Sherrell (Richmond: John Knox Press, 1971), pp. 32–33.

17. Stimpson, p. 475.

18. Greer, pp. 314, 326, 313.

19. Betty Roszak, "The Human Continuum," in *Masculine/Feminine*, p. 300.

20. Dixon, p. 198.

21. Hacker, p. 142.

22. Paul H. Douglas, "Three Saints in Politics," *American Scholar*, Vol. 40, No. 2 (Spring 1971).

23. Hacker, p. 142.

24. Theodore Roszak, pp. 99–100.

25. Betty Roszak, p. 302.

26. Greer, p. 136.

27. Kathy Mulherin and Jennifer Gardner, "Growing Up a Woman," *Christianity and Crisis*, Vol. 30, No. 16 (October 5, 1970), p. 208.

28. Greer, pp. 319, 318.

29. *Ibid.*, pp. 286, 287, 322.

30. Judith Benninger Brown, "Female Liberation First, and Now," in *Masculine/Feminine*, p. 224.

Notes

31. Alice Rossi, "Sex Equality: The Beginning of Ideology," in *Masculine/Feminine*, pp. 179 ff.
32. Glendy Culligan, "Born Free But Not Liberated," *Saturday Review*, Vol. 54, No. 23 (June 5, 1971), p. 41.
33. Joreen, p. 276.

2. Vive la Différence?

1. Greer, pp. 50–51.
2. Mary Daly, *The Church and the Second Sex* (New York: Harper & Row, 1968), chapter 4.
3. Estelle Ramey, "Well, Fellows, What Did Happen at the Bay of Pigs? And Who Was in Control?" *McCall's*, Vol. 98, No. 4 (January 1971), pp. 81, 26.
4. Norman Mailer, *The Prisoner of Sex* (Boston: Little, Brown and Co., 1971), p. 61.
5. Jonathan Yardley, "Women's Lib Gets Rough," review of *Sexual Politics* by Kate Millett, *The New Republic*, Vol. 163, No. 5 (August 1, 1970), p. 31.
6. Sidney Cornelia Callahan, *The Illusion of Eve: Modern Woman's Quest for Identity* (New York: Sheed and Ward, 1965), p. 81 (italics mine).
7. Greer, p. 10.
8. Naomi Weisstein, "Kinder, Küche, Kirche as Scientific Law: Psychology Constructs the Female," *motive*, Vol. 29, Nos. 6 & 7 (March-April 1969), p. 78.
9. Robert Reinhold, *Louisville Courier-Journal*, September 7, 1970.
10. Jo Freeman, "The Social Construction of the Second Sex," in *Women and Society*, ed. Diana Reische (New York: The H. W. Wilson Co., 1972), p. 135.
11. Callahan, p. 78.
12. Carlyle Marney, "The Christian Community and the Homosexual," in *Moral Issues and Christian Response*, ed. Paul T. Jersild and Dale A. Johnson (New York: Holt, Rinehart and Winston, 1971), p. 185.
13. C. S. Lewis, *De Descriptione Temporum: An Inaugural Lecture* (Cambridge: At the University Press, 1955), p. 15.
14. Ramey, p. 81.
15. F. J. J. Buytendijk, *La Femme* (Brussels, 1954).
16. Edmund W. Overstreet, "Biological Make-up of Woman," in *The Potential of Woman*, ed. Seymour M. Farber and Roger H. L. Wilson (New York: McGraw-Hill Book Co., 1963), pp. 15, 16.
17. Ramey, p. 81.

18. Nancy R. McWilliams, "Feminism and Femininity," *Commonweal*, Vol. 92, No. 9 (May 15, 1970), p. 220.
19. Ashley Montagu, *The Natural Superiority of Women*, rev. ed. (New York: The Macmillan Co., 1968), p. 49.
20. Vance Packard, *The Sexual Wilderness* (New York: David McKay Co., 1968), p. 399.
21. *Ibid.*, pp. 401, 403, 402.
22. *Ibid.*, p. 401.
23. John Money, "Developmental Differentiation of Femininity and Masculinity Compared," in *The Potential of Woman*, pp. 58, 59.
24. Packard, p. 401.
25. McWilliams, p. 221.
26. Packard, p. 402.
27. Diana Trilling, "Female Biology in a Male Culture," *Saturday Review*, Vol. 53, No. 41 (October 10, 1970), p. 17.
28. Benjamin Spock, "The Question of Psychological Differences Between the Sexes," in *Women and Society*, pp. 157–158.
29. Erik H. Erikson, *Identity: Youth and Crisis* (New York: W. W. Norton & Co., 1968), pp. 266–267, 275.
30. *Ibid.*, pp. 268 ff.; see also "Configurations in Play—Clinical Notes," *Psychoanalytic Quarterly*, Vol. 6 (1937), pp. 139–214; *Gandhi's Truth* (New York: W. W. Norton & Co., 1969).
31. David C. McClelland, "Wanted: A New Self-Image for Women," in *Dialogue on Women*, ed. Robert Theobald (Indianapolis: Bobbs-Merrill Co., 1967), p. 45.
32. Packard, p. 340.
33. Abby Stitt, "Will Boys Be Boys? and Girls, Girls?" *Mother's Manual*, November-December 1970, p. 28.
34. McClelland, p. 43.
35. *Ibid.*, p. 46.
36. Montagu, pp. 92–93, 86–87; Robert Deitz, *Louisville Courier-Journal and Times*, May 31, 1970.
37. Greer, pp. 279, 273.
38. Montagu, pp. 91–92, 67.
39. Meryle Secrest, *Louisville Courier-Journal*, February 10, 1971.
40. Robert J. Lifton, *History and Human Survival* (New York: Random House, 1970), pp. 260, 265.
41. Lynn White, Jr., *Educating Our Daughters: A Challenge to the Colleges* (New York: Harper & Brothers, 1950), pp. 41–44.
42. Eleanor E. Maccoby, "Women's Intellect," in *The Potential of Woman*, pp. 24 ff.; see also Freeman, pp. 125 ff.

43. Judith M. Bardwick and Elizabeth Douvan, "Ambivalence: The Socialization of Women," in *Woman in Sexist Society*, pp. 148–149.
44. Karl Stern, *The Flight from Woman* (New York: Farrar, Straus and Giroux, 1965), chapter 3.
45. *Ibid.*, pp. 35, 21–23.
46. Alan Watts, "The Woman in Man," in *The Potential of Woman*, pp. 80 ff.
47. Greer, pp. 100–107.
48. Quoted in Greer, p. 103.
49. Ann Belford Ulanov, *The Feminine: in Jungian Psychology and in Christian Theology* (Evanston: Northwestern University Press, 1971), pp. 141, 145, 148. Used by permission.
50. *Ibid.*, p. 26.
51. *Ibid.*, pp. 12–13 (italics mine).
52. *Ibid.*, pp. 21–29.
53. *Ibid.*, p. 29.
54. *Ibid.*, pp. 32–34.
55. *Ibid.*, pp. 35–38, 41.
56. *Ibid.*, pp. 39, 40, 43.
57. *Ibid.*, p. 246.
58. *Ibid.*, p. 47.
59. *Ibid.*, p. 49.
60. *Ibid.*, p. 66.
61. *Ibid.*, pp. 67–69.
62. *Ibid.*, p. 243.
63. *Ibid.*, p. 69.
64. *Ibid.*, p. 70.
65. *Ibid.*, p. 255.
66. *Ibid.*, pp. 267–268.
67. *Ibid.*, p. 268.
68. *Ibid.*, p. 272.
69. *Ibid.*, pp. 268–269.
70. *Ibid.*, p. 197.
71. Betty Rollin, "Backlash Against Women's Lib," in *Women and Society*, p. 31.
72. Ulanov, p. 207.
73. *Ibid.*, pp. 134, 163.
74. *Ibid.*, p. 146.
75. *Ibid.*, pp. 154–155, 157–160.
76. *Ibid.*, pp. 168–169, 172–175.

77. *Ibid.*, p. 184.
78. Betty Friedan, "Beyond Women's Liberation," *McCall's*, Vol. 99, No. 11 (August 1971), pp. 82 ff.
79. Mailer, p. 60.
80. Herbert W. Richardson, *Nun, Witch, Playmate: The Americanization of Sex* (New York: Harper & Row, 1971), p. 89.
81. *Masculine/Feminine*, Foreword, p. vii.
82. Callahan, p. 85.
83. Richardson, pp. 54–57, 38–40.
84. Rollo May, *Love and Will* (New York: W. W. Norton & Co., 1969), p. 54.
85. McWilliams, p. 221.
86. Simone de Beauvoir, *The Second Sex* (New York: Alfred A. Knopf, 1952), p. 688.
87. A. H. Maslow, "Love in Self-Actualizing People," *Sexual Behavior and Personality Characteristics*, ed. Manfred DeMartino (New York: Grove Press, 1963), p. 152.
88. Sidney Cornelia Callahan, *Exiled to Eden: The Christian Experience of Sex* (New York: Sheed and Ward, 1968), p. 52. (This book was originally titled *Beyond Birth Control*.)
89. Maguire, p. 80.
90. Harvey Cox, "The Virgin and the Dynamo Revisited," *Humanities, Religion and the Arts Tomorrow*, ed. Howard Hunter (New York: Holt, Rinehart & Winston, 1972), p. 31.
91. Friedan, p. 83.
92. James B. Nelson, *Moral Nexus: Ethics of Christian Identity and Community* (Philadelphia: The Westminster Press, 1971), p. 102.
93. Trilling, p. 18.
94. Callahan, *Exiled to Eden*, p. 231.
95. Daly, p. 130.
96. Freeman, p. 128.
97. Nancy Chodorow, "Being and Doing: A Cross-Cultural Examination of the Socialization of Males and Females," in *Woman in Sexist Society*, p. 193.
98. Callahan, *Exiled to Eden*, pp. 121–122.
99. Callahan, *The Illusion of Eve*, p. 135.
100. Gloria Steinem, "What It Would Be Like If Women Win," in *Women and Society*, p. 222.
101. "The New Fathers," *Life*, Vol. 73, No. 2 (July 14, 1972), p. 70.

3. Man on the Make and on the Run

1. Karen Horney, "Distrust Between the Sexes," in *Masculine/Feminine*, pp. 111 ff.
2. Mailer, pp. 116, 111.
3. Rosemary Ruether, "Women's Liberation in Historical and Theological Perspective," *Soundings*, Vol. 53, No. 4 (Winter 1970), p. 364.
4. *Ibid.*, p. 366.
5. Richardson, pp. 4–7.
6. *Ibid.*, pp. 7 ff.
7. Albert Camus, *The Fall* (New York: Alfred A. Knopf, 1956), pp. 44–45.
8. Richard Gilman, "Where Did It All Go Wrong?" *Life*, Vol. 71, No. 7 (August 13, 1971), p. 54.
9. Callahan, *Exiled to Eden*, p. 222.
10. Rosemary Ruether, "Mother Earth and the Megamachine," *Christianity and Crisis*, Vol. 31, No. 21 (December 13, 1971), p. 269.
11. Ruether, "Women's Liberation in Historical and Theological Perspective," p. 365; "Mother Earth and the Megamachine," p. 270.
12. Richardson, pp. 22, 11–12.
13. Herbert W. Richardson, "Evolution of Virginity," *Church and Society*, Vol. 60, No. 4 (March-April 1970), pp. 7–11.
14. John H. Hayes, *Introduction to the Bible* (Philadelphia: The Westminster Press, 1971), pp. 89–91.
15. *Ibid.*, p. 91.
16. Ruether, "Mother Earth and the Megamachine," p. 270.
17. Penelope Washbourne (Chen), "Rediscovering the Feminine in God," *The Tower* (alumni magazine of Union Theological Seminary), Vol. 17, No. 3 (Spring 1971).
18. Ruether, "Mother Earth and the Megamachine," p. 267.
19. *Ibid.*, p. 270.
20. Richardson, *Nun, Witch, Playmate*, pp. 61, 64.
21. Lynn White, Jr., "The Historical Roots of Our Ecologic Crisis," *Science*, Vol. 155, No. 3767 (March 10, 1967), p. 1204.
22. *Ibid.*, p. 1205.
23. Alan W. Watts, *Nature, Man, and Woman* (New York: Random House, Vintage Books, 1970), p. 52.

24. *Ibid.*, p. 44.
25. Rosemary Ruether, "An Unexpected Tribute to the Theologian," *Theology Today*, Vol. 27, No. 3 (October 1970), pp. 337 ff.
26. Frederick Elder, *Crisis in Eden: A Religious Study of Man and Environment* (Nashville: Abingdon Press, 1970), pp. 83–89.
27. White, *Educating Our Daughters*, p. 74.
28. Richardson, *Nun, Witch, Playmate*, p. 69.
29. Michael Novak, *Ascent of the Mountain, Flight of the Dove: An Invitation to Religious Studies* (New York: Harper & Row, 1971), pp. 111–112.
30. Stern, p. 229.
31. *Ibid.*, pp. 1–3.
32. Quoted in *Time*, June 8, 1970, p. 49.
33. Stern, p. 138.
34. *Ibid.*, p. 76.
35. *Ibid.*, p. 288.
36. *Ibid.*, p. 300.
37. Watts, *Nature, Man, and Woman*, pp. 154–155.
38. Ruby R. Leavitt, "Women in Other Cultures," in *Woman in Sexist Society*, pp. 276 ff.
39. Theodore Roszak, p. 92.
40. Ulanov, pp. 260–261.
41. May, p. 46.
42. Duane Mehl, "Sex in the Future," *motive*, Vol. 27, No. 1 (October 1966), p. 28.
43. May, p. 54.
44. *Ibid.*, p. 45.
45. *Ibid.*, p. 16.
46. Montagu, p. 49.
47. Renatus Hartogs with Hans Fantel, *Four-Letter Word Games* (New York: Dell Publishing Co., 1967), pp. 150–151.
48. Packard, p. 179.
49. Stanley Kauffmann, "Public Privates," *The New Republic*, Vol. 163, No. 2 (July 11, 1970), pp. 32–33.
50. Constantina Safilios-Rothschild, *Toward a Sociology of Women* (Lexington, Mass.: Xerox College Publishing, 1972), p. 102.
51. Lillian Roxon, "The Intelligent Woman's Guide to Sex Manuals," *Mademoiselle*, Vol. 73, No. 3 (July 1971).
52. *Ibid.*, p. 156.
53. *Ibid.*
54. Susan Edmiston and Mitzi Haggard, "Germaine Greer: Two Views (View I)," *Pageant*, Vol. 27 (September 1971), p. 18.

55. Greer, p. 34.
56. Peter Michelson, "An Apology for Pornography," *The New Republic*, Vol. 155, No. 24 (December 10, 1966), p. 22.
57. *Ibid.*, p. 24.
58. R. C. Erickson, "Sex as the Writer's New Myth," *The Christian Century*, Vol. 82, No. 20 (May 19, 1965), p. 642.
59. Robert Detweiler, *"The Elements of John Updike:* Another Appraisal," *Newsletter of the Conference on Christianity and Literature*, Vol. 20, No. 4 (Summer 1971), p. 27 (italics mine).
60. Melvin Maddocks, "Big News: Pure Sex Is Not Enough . . . ," review of *Providence Island* by Calder Willingham, *Life*, Vol. 66, No. 6 (February 14, 1969), p. 10.
61. Ingrid Bengis, "Heavy Combat in the Erogenous Zone," *The Village Voice*, August 13, 1970.
62. *Ibid.*, p. 5.
63. Roxon, p. 157.
64. Stern, p. 286.
65. Ulanov, pp. 290, 307.
66. *Ibid.*, pp. 303–304.
67. *Ibid.*, pp. 330–331.
68. *Ibid.*, p. 304.
69. *Ibid.*, p. 316.
70. Irene Marinoff, "The Erosion of the Mystery," in *New Theology No. 7*, ed. Martin E. Marty and Dean G. Peerman (New York: The Macmillan Co., 1970), p. 32.
71. *Ibid.*, p. 31.
72. Phyllis Chesler, "Patient and Patriarch: Women in the Psychotherapeutic Relationship," in *Woman in Sexist Society*, pp. 260 ff.
73. Valerie Saiving Goldstein, "The Human Situation: A Feminine View," *The Journal of Religion*, Vol. 40, No. 2 (April 1960), pp. 100–112.
74. Quoted in Rollin, p. 32.
75. Margaret Adams, "The Compassion Trap," in *Woman in Sexist Society*, pp. 401 ff.
76. Montagu, p. 104.
77. Erikson, pp. 293–294.
78. Ruether, "An Unexpected Tribute to the Theologian," p. 336.
79. *Ibid.*
80. Sam Keen, *Apology for Wonder* (New York: Harper & Row, 1969), pp. 87–90.
81. Novak, p. 25.

82. *Ibid.*, p. 209.
83. Keen, p. 146.
84. Erikson, pp. 261–262.
85. White, *Educating Our Daughters*, pp. 48–49.
86. McClelland, p. 45.

4. Toward a More "Feminine" Future

1. Rossi, pp. 180–184.
2. Marilyn Bowers, "Women's Liberation: A Catholic View," *Theology Today*, Vol. 28, No. 1 (April 1971), p. 33.
3. James J. White, "Women in Law," in *Toward a Sociology of Women*, pp. 277 ff.
4. Trilling, p. 18.
5. Martha S. White, "Psychological and Social Barriers to Women in Science," in *Toward a Sociology of Women*, p. 314.
6. *Ibid.*, p. 312.
7. Rossi, p. 184.
8. Jean Mayer, "Let's Put Women in Their Place—Like, for Instance, City Hall," *McCall's*, Vol. 98, No. 5 (February 1971), pp. 74 ff.
9. Erikson, pp. 262, 292–293; see also Montagu, pp. 33–34, 56–58.
10. Trilling, p. 18.
11. Morgan, p. 244.
12. Ruether, "Mother Earth and the Megamachine," pp. 271–272.
13. Barbara Bovee Polk, "Women's Liberation: Movement for Equality," in *Toward a Sociology of Women*, p. 322.
14. Greer, p. 108.
15. Quoted in William Braden, *The Age of Aquarius: Technology and the Cultural Revolution* (Chicago: Quadrangle Books, 1970), p. 190.
16. Lifton, pp. 271–272.
17. *Ibid.*, pp. 284–285.
18. Muriel Castanis, "Behind Every Artist There's a Penis," *The Village Voice*, March 19, 1970.
19. Rossi, p. 184.
20. *Louisville Courier-Journal*, August 24, 1971.
21. Marion Meade, *Louisville Courier-Journal*, April 18, 1971.
22. Morgan, pp. 245, 246.
23. Charles A. Reich, *The Greening of America* (New York: Random House, 1970), pp. 295, 305, 316.
24. *Ibid.*, pp. 351, 352, 370, 390.

25. Braden, p. 164.
26. *Ibid.*, pp. 192–193.
27. Sam Keen, "Manifesto for a Dionysian Theology," in *New Theology No. 7*, p. 102; *Apology for Wonder*, pp. 193–194.
28. Callahan, *Exiled to Eden*, pp. 22–23.
29. *Ibid.*, p. 68.
30. Keen, *Apology for Wonder*, pp. 190–191.
31. *Ibid.*, p. 197.
32. Callahan, *Exiled to Eden*, p. 137.
33. *Ibid.*, p. 49.
34. *Ibid.*, p. 38.
35. May, pp. 72 ff.
36. *Ibid.*, pp. 37–38, 317–320.
37. Richardson, *Nun, Witch, Playmate*, pp. 105–107.
38. Braden, pp. 204–205.
39. Keen, *Apology for Wonder*, p. 145.
40. Maslow, p. 153.
41. Keen, *Apology for Wonder*, p. 146.
42. Hartogs, p. 151.
43. *Ibid.*, pp. 150–151.
44. Tom F. Driver, "On Taking Sex Seriously," *Christianity and Crisis*, Vol. 23, No. 17 (October 14, 1963), p. 177.
45. Natalie Shainess, "I Don't Regard Sex as Fun . . . ," *Mademoiselle*, Vol. 73, No. 3 (July 1971).
46. Keen, *Apology for Wonder*, p. 142.
47. Quoted in "Gloria Steinem: A Liberated Woman Despite Beauty, Chic and Success," *Newsweek*, Vol. 78, No. 7 (August 16, 1971), p. 54.
48. Shainess, p. 78.
49. Alvin Toffler, *Future Shock* (New York: Random House, 1970), pp. 221–222.
50. Benjamin Spock, "Children and Their Families," in *Women and Society*, p. 193.
51. Discussed in Leighton McCutchen, "The Father Figure in Psychology and Religion," *Journal of the American Academy of Religion*, Vol. 40, No. 2 (June 1972), pp. 185–186, as based on Bruno Bettelheim, *Children of the Dream* (New York: The Macmillan Co., 1969).
52. Myrna Blyth, "Raising a Bright and Happy Child," in *Women and Society*, pp. 177 ff.
53. Toffler, p. 212.

54. Harvey Cox, "Eight Theses on Female Liberation," *Christianity and Crisis*, Vol. 31, No. 16 (October 4, 1971), p. 200.
55. *Ibid.*, p. 201.
56. *Ibid.*
57. Amitai Etzioni, "The Women's Movement—Tokens vs. Objectives," *Saturday Review*, Vol. 55, No. 21 (May 20, 1972), p. 35.
58. Bowers, p. 31.
59. Mary Daly, "After the Death of God the Father," *Commonweal*, Vol. 94, No. 1 (March 12, 1971), p. 10.
60. May, p. 105.
61. "Circumstance," *The Christian Century*, Vol. 88, No. 21 (May 26, 1971), p. 648.
62. Ulanov, p. 135.
63. Washbourne, p. 9.
64. *Ibid.*, p. 12.
65. Keen, "Manifesto for a Dionysian Theology," p. 102.
66. Washbourne, p. 12.
67. Norman Pittenger, "Process Theology Revisited," *Theology Today*, Vol. 27, No. 2 (July 1970), p. 212.
68. Alfred North Whitehead, *Process and Reality* (New York: The Macmillan Co., 1929), p. 532.
69. John B. Cobb, Jr., *God and the World* (Philadelphia: The Westminster Press, 1969), p. 90.
70. Carol Christ and Marilyn Collins, "Shattering the Idols of Men: Theology from the Perspective of Women's Experience," *Reflection*, Vol. 69, No. 4 (May 1972), p. 14.
71. Whitehead, pp. 519–520.
72. *Ibid.*, pp. 520–521.
73. White, "The Historical Roots of Our Ecologic Crisis," p. 1206.
74. Joseph H. Fichter, "Holy Father Church," *Commonweal*, Vol. 92, No. 9 (May 15, 1970), p. 218.